MAKING MORE *of* MARRIAGE

John & Anne Coles

First published in Great Britain in 2000 by
new wine international publishing
4A Ridley Avenue, Ealing, London W13 9XW
ISBN 1 902977 07 6

First Edition 2000
Reprinted 2005

A catalogue record for this book is available from the British Library

Typeset & cover design by The Design Chapel
Cover photography Shu Tomioka
Printed in Great Britain by Biddles Ltd.

To Audrey and Geoffrey, Ruth and John,
who lived it out before us.

If marriage is the best thing on earth you can
give to your children this is for you,
Laura, Beth, David and Simon.

CONTENTS

Foreword

Acknowledgements

In the Beginning   1

1   Choosing to Love   13

2   Leaving the Past   23

3   Celebrating Differences   37

4   Recognising Roles   51

5   Communicating Love   63

6   Resolving Conflict   75

7   Satisfying Sex   95

8   Looking Outwards   113

9   Managing Money   131

10   Enjoying Romance   145

Conclusion   159

Foreword

I have just finished reading this book on marriage and I am so delighted with the wholesome way John and Anne Coles deal with a subject which is being so undermined in society today. It is easy to read, funny and frank where it's appropriate, personal and practical - we can all profit from reading it.

John and Anne are both highly respected leaders and speakers and communicate meaningfully. They are hosts at New Wine and John will be taking over as Director. They take training days, leadership gatherings and clergy retreats all over the world. They have been married for many years and have two sons and two daughters in their teens and over.

This book is a must for couples getting married and is the kind of book that should be re-read every three years by those who are already married. This is also a book about sex - yes - but marriage is much more than sex - its about a relationship. There is a lot here to teach us. I believe they have got marriage into the perspective that God ordained for it. Marriage is not a sacrament of the gospel but it is certainly a wonderful means of Grace.

David Pytches

Acknowledgements

There are many people we want to thank for making this book possible. David and Mary Pytches motivated us to 'go for it'; we are also indebted to David for taking the time to read the manuscript and for his wise and helpful comments. David and Jenny Rosser have been the most patient and good-humoured of publishers. Thank you too to all the staff and members of St. B.s who gave us the peace and encouragement to keep going until it was finished. We are grateful to Shu Tomioka, who provided the photos for the cover and to Kathy Pavey for typing up the seminar transcripts.

Last but not least thank you to Laura, Beth, David and Simon for bearing with as we wrote and being such fun to relax with afterwards!

John & Anne Coles June 2000

In the Beginning

A ripple of laughter ran round the congregation. We wondered what caused it. We were kneeling before the Bishop as he prayed for God's blessing on our marriage. We had just made the most important vows of our lives. We had just paid each other the biggest compliment any human being ever makes to another. We had said that we were committing ourselves to love each other through thick and thin, 'for better for worse, for richer for poorer, in sickness and in health, till death us do part'. It was only after the service that we discovered the reason for the laughter. Earlier in the day John had responded to his best man's offer of help by giving him his shoes to clean. As we knelt at the head of the church, our family and friends could see the soles of his shoes; on the left were two large white letters HE, and on the right were the matching two LP!

HELP is probably a most appropriate prayer at such a time. When we make such promises we have no idea what the future holds, no idea how we might change, or how the person we are marrying might change. We might well wonder how anyone could think of making such sweeping promises when most people find it hard to keep New Year Resolutions beyond the second week of January! Perhaps for this reason fewer young people are committing themselves to each other in marriage nowadays. Where is the help to come from should they ever need it?

We made those promises on July 23rd 1977. We still believe that marriage is a glorious gift from God enriching the lives of those to whom he gives it. In the Bible story of creation in Genesis God sees the loneliness of the man he has created and says 'It is not good for the man to be alone. I will make a helper suitable for him.' (Gen 2:18) To enable human beings to enjoy all that God intends the story goes on: 'For this reason a man will leave his father and mother and be united to his wife, and they will become one flesh'. (Gen 2:24)

Why write?

The reason we are writing this book is because we believe in marriage. After 23 years we are enjoying more than ever the marriage that God has given us.

Both of us are children of happily married parents. We owe an enormous debt of gratitude to them because they taught us by their lives how to be married and make it work. We lived with them day in, day out and watched it, absorbed it, experienced it and grew up believing in it! If a happy marriage is the best gift that you can give your children, they gave us the best. We, in turn want the best for our children too.

We are not marriage counsellors in the professionally trained sense. Much of what we have learned has also come from those who have shared their stories with us as church pastors in an effort to find a better way through their difficulties. As we have talked and prayed with them we have seen God bless those who face the obstacles with faith and courage. We thank them too. Where they have allowed us to use their stories in the course of this book we have changed names and minor details in order to preserve their identities.

We have tried to live our lives on the basis of Jesus' command to his first disciples 'Freely you have received, freely give'.(Matt 10:8).

If we are able to pass any of this on to help others to enjoy the marriage God has given them we will be delighted. It is in that vein that we write.

Pray Now

You are probably reading this book because you want God to enrich the marriage he has given you. Why not pray right now that God will do that! God is able to do 'immeasurably more than all we ask or imagine, according to his power that is at work within us.' (Eph 3:20)

Prayer

Heavenly Father,
Thank you for our marriage and for all the joy that it has brought to our lives.
Thank you that marriage is your idea and that you are committed to seeing it work.
Thank you too that you have promised to help us find a way through the difficulties.
Please make us more like Jesus so that we will better strengthen and encourage each other.
We ask too that you will bless us as we read this book.
Shine the light of your holy Spirit into our lives, that our marriage would more fully reflect your glory.
For Jesus' sake, Amen.

What's the point?

From recent research work it seems people really benefit from marriage. This is interesting at a time when young people in the UK seem to find it harder than ever to enter into lifelong committed relationships. They don't seem to know what they could be missing!

3

Guarantee of happiness

According to recent research by Prof. Michael Argyle, Emeritus Reader in Happiness at Oxford one of the most important guarantees of happiness, especially with men, is marriage. After analysing thousands of detailed questionnaires Prof. Argyle concluded: 'Marriage provides companionship, particularly during leisure time, and a great deal of emotional help and support - especially for men'. 'Husbands are not very good listeners. But they seem to need it (marriage) more than women.' The least happy are the divorced or separated, who are even more miserable than people who have been widowed. Extra-marital affairs tend to bring unhappiness, because of the damage they do the marriage. 'Having two people who give you support and company could be a good thing - but it rarely works out that way.' (The Sunday Telegraph 1 Oct 1998)

Married people are healthier

Married people spend half as much time sick and in hospital as single people, says a Dutch scientist. Dr Inez Joung carried out a survey among singles, marrieds, divorced, widowed and those co-habiting and found that 'married people were healthier than any of the others, particularly divorced people, who suffered from 30% more chronic conditions'. The support that married couples give to one another is a major reason for their better health, but men, it seems, rely on this more than women, who have a better network of family and friends. Single men also suffer more than single women because of their tendency not to take as good care of themselves. (CEN 31 May 1996)

Children benefit too

The Exeter Family Study, conducted by Dr John Tripp and Marcia Cockett of the Department of Child Health at Exeter University's postgraduate medical school, demonstrates quite clearly that the children of divorced parents are more likely to be unhappy, unhealthy and handicapped at school than the children of parents who quarrel but remain married. The children from 'reordered families' (divorcing parents remarrying) were more than twice as likely as the others to think badly of themselves, to have problems with school work and making friends, to wet their beds, and have repeated bouts of illness, (often psychosomatic), and to describe themselves simply as being miserable most of the time. As for those whose families had been reordered more than once, they were more than ten times more likely to have a low opinion of themselves. The researchers were firm; it was not poverty, or conflict, or anything except the fact of losing a parent that did the damage. (The Times 9 Feb 1994)

Good for Society

The impact of this research is at least this. Marriage is the bedrock of a happy society. If we neglect our marriages and allow them to fall into disrepair there will be a huge cost to pay; in the loss of our own happiness; in the cost to our children; and in the cost to our society in terms of health service, and additional care and education for children from dysfunctional families. It is probably in recognition of the impact of marriage on society, as much as from a desire to enforce a specifically Christian lifestyle on a predominantly non-Christian culture that James Jones, the Bishop of Liverpool, recently called for the appointment of a Minister for the Family.

No bed of roses

To say that marriage is God's gift and generally brings happiness to us is not to say that it is always a bed of roses! God may have intended that but the result of the Fall is that every good gift from God has been so twisted by the enemy that to get the best out of anything requires hard work. You only have to look at our garden to see that we aren't always prepared to put in the hard work which would enable us to get the best from what God has given! Marriage is between two imperfect people living in an imperfect world. Even though the most romantic of us, blinded by love, might think we are marrying a perfect partner the experience of a few years, or even days, of marriage proves otherwise! The consequence is that we won't always feel deliriously happy. There will almost inevitably be high points and low points within every couple's marriage.

Paul Tournier, the Catholic writer on marriage says in his book 'Marriage Difficulties' (SCM Press 1967) 'You have problems? That's quite normal; all couples do. As a matter of fact it is a good thing. Those who make a success of their marriage are those who tackle their problems together and who overcome them. Those who lack the courage to do this are the ones whose marriage is a failure.'

Anne writes: Our marriage has gone through some ups and downs and probably one of the low points for me was about six years and two children into our marriage. When we married, it was as committed Christians and our spiritual life was a very important part of our marriage. However one Easter John found himself crying out to God for more power in his life and ministry and as a result he was overwhelmed by the Holy Spirit. He didn't actually say very much about it, probably because it was all so intense and personal, in fact, he didn't realise he'd 'become charismatic' because we didn't have all the right words for things at that stage, but I realised that he had started praying in tongues. That in itself was a huge blow to me; here was something I could no longer share with him since it was not part of my experience and further, I had always assumed that people who prayed in tongues were either weird or emotionally vulnerable and now I faced the reality that I was married to one of those people!

As far as I could see we would never agree spiritually again, our blissful togetherness was now threatened and our marriage would

6

become an empty shell. And the worst thing was that I was married to a Vicar - if I divorced him it would ruin his career and I wouldn't have a house! That dreadful prospect forced me onto my knees before God and that was the beginning of the solution. God lovingly and patiently listened as I poured out my woes, He brought me face to face with the truth of my wrong attitudes, forgave me and gave me hope that there was a future! How John and I then worked it through together and in so doing found a deeper relationship with each other is simply another example of how marriage progresses through the downs as well as the ups! Maybe you are right now at one of those low points in the life of your marriage. If so we want to encourage you that with God's help and your commitment it can get better and you can get through it.

 Talking point:

Recall together the times when you have been most happy in your marriage.

Marital Satisfaction

Below is a graph of marital satisfaction throughout our life career. It starts off at a very high point. At the beginning of our married life together, we're in love, we make time for one another and our relationship blossoms, but as we get to the child bearing period couples commonly experience a low; perhaps pregnancy has meant physical discomfort for the wife, then the new infant arrives and after the initial excitement has died down we discover that our nights or days are totally absorbed in caring for the new addition, added to which the husband no longer has a wife who thinks he's the summit of her existence, there's competition around!

Husbands' and Wives' Marital Satisfaction Over the Family Career

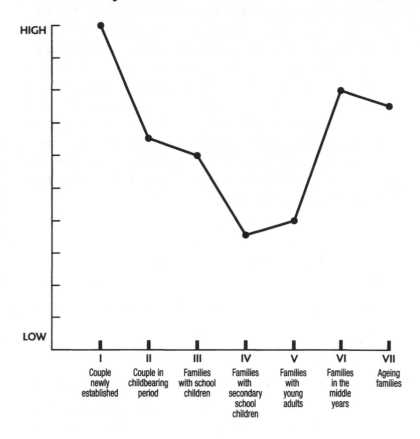

Then there is continuing pressure during the time of growing family responsibility with energetic primary schoolchildren and moody teenagers. If that is the stage you are in as you read this and you are thinking 'I can't say that I'm madly, truly, deeply, in love', it may be that part of what you are experiencing is the normal numbing effect of busyness. You are responding to the demands of raising children, the managing of home life, the pressures of work life, and if you're a Christian you may well have the call of church life too. It seems as if everyone wants you to be a house group leader, a worship leader, make the coffee and run the Sunday school! Life is so incredibly busy that you hardly have time for yourself, let alone one another. Then those small children with their endless capacity for daytime activity are suddenly teenagers who stay up later at night than their parents! Since most parents are out all day working, (to fund the teenager's clothing allowance!) they don't see each other during the day but neither do they see each other alone in the evening,- in fact they don't even sleep at night because they're awake wondering when their children are going to come home!

Don't despair for your marriage though, enjoy the children as they grow up because when those teenagers become young adults you'll find that marital satisfaction begins to go up again. All of a sudden there are a few spaces in our calendar and the marriage relationship needs to be nourished and restocked in order to face the next stage of life.

With the onset of retirement there are new pressures as well as new opportunities. The arrival of an elderly and infirm parent in the home can bring another drain on time and patience and stretch the resources of our marriage, so we need to take stock again and determine to give some time to our relationship.

God's idea

Marriage is God's idea and His idea is that it should be lifelong. That means your marriage is God's idea for you and if it's God's idea for you then it means it's possible for you. Through all the changes of our lives, at all the different stages and ages, God has a plan for our best.

Someone has coined the phrase 'marriage is made in Heaven, but man is responsible for the maintenance work'. While there is much truth in that, we also need to know that God doesn't just create marriage but he sustains it.

This book

We have included material gleaned from both our reading and experience. We hope you find this as interesting and helpful as we have. We have used most of the material either in seminars at the New Wine summer events at Shepton Mallet or in courses on Preparing for Marriage or Marriage Enrichment at our church.

One thing we have found invaluable in our marriage is a sense of humour. Being able to laugh together is fun and releasing. To this end we have peppered the text of the book with quips and jokes. They are not meant to be taken seriously. Additionally there are pithy comments for you to chew over.

Since marriage is God's idea, He wants to bless every couple who commit themselves to loving each other for life! The principles behind a good marriage are the same for all of us. Although this book is written with Christians in mind, we are aware that not every Christian has a spouse who would want to be called a Christian and not every couple reading this will have made a commitment to Jesus Christ. We hope that you will still read on and find the chapters helpful.

Psychologists say that it takes at least 8 weeks to change any significant behaviour habits. If you are reading this book because you know that significant changes need to be made for you to make more of your marriage, then we suggest that you try reading this book together at the rate of a chapter a week. Try setting aside an evening each week to read the chapter, fill in any questionnaires, discuss together the 'Talking Points' and address the feelings that are raised. It may be a good idea to tell some friends that you are doing this so that they are able to pray for you as you do this. Beware: a husband cannot change his wife's behaviour, nor a wife her husband's. Each one of us needs to take responsibility for change in ourselves.

It says in Proverbs 18 :22 'He who finds a wife finds what is good and receives favour from the Lord'. God intends us to experience that favour, not just at the start of a marriage, but favour continuing throughout a marriage. Additionally this text tells us that God is willing to pour his sustaining grace into our lives to enable us to experience his goodness through this gift of marital satisfaction lifelong.

So at whatever stage you find yourself as you read this book, be encouraged that God is committed to helping you to make more of the marriage He has given you.

CHAPTER 1

Choosing to love

Most people will probably agree that love is the basis of a good marriage. What there is disagreement over is the nature of love. John recalls the agony of knowing whether or when it was right to say to Anne 'I love you'. While knowing this should be the right thing to say to the girl I was going out with, I wasn't really sure what it meant. Nor was I sure whether the feeling I had was a sufficiently strong feeling to sustain a marriage - or at that stage to pop the question 'will you marry me?'.

Many do not go through this agony in their courtship but sadly face it some years later within their marriage. The question is then 'do I love this person enough to stay married to him/her?' If there is little understanding about the character of true marriage-sustaining love at that stage then the glue that holds the marriage together begins to weaken. Divorce is easily contemplated if all that has held a marriage together is the intoxicating feeling of 'being in love'.

Falling in love

All the world loves a lover, so the saying goes. Even the most sexually voracious idols of our time can turn out to be romantics at heart. These newspaper headlines caught our attention in 1996: 'I preached Free Love but I only wanted one woman - my wife' (Daily Mail 12 Oct 1996). The writer was none other than Donovan, singing icon of the free-loving 60's. He had discovered that his outward behaviour did not satisfy his inner desires for staying in love with the woman he had decided to marry.

Almost all films and stories with a 'love content' are focused around the events leading to a couple falling in love. No sooner have the pair in question been brought together, declared their love for each other and overcome all obstacles to being united, than the picture fades and we are left assuming that they will live 'happily ever after' in the same state that we left them. It is easy to see how the assumption that the 'falling in love experience' lasts forever has gripped our culture.

Falling in love is certainly one of life's precious experiences and the spine-tingling memories of it can be recaptured fondly years later. However we were never meant to keep 'falling'! The phrase 'the course of true love -' indicates that true love should be a developing and deepening thing. The candid observation of the proverb is that the course of true love never runs smooth. The purpose of this book is to help us to 'stay' in love.

What happens when we fall in love? There are a number of common characteristics belonging to the experience of falling in love, and the euphoria that surrounds it. These are most frequently effortlessness, obsession, illusion, sexual arousal and self-pleasing.

Effortlessness

You will probably remember some of those early feelings of being in love. There was an effortlessness about being together. Every minute together was treasured - every conversation was nectar - every phone call was such a delight that even the (surprisingly- large) bill was bearable! A young friend of ours who is usually tacit and monosyllabic in conversation can without difficulty spend an hour and a half talking to his latest girlfriend on the phone. Preplanning of activities together was not really necessary because simply being together was a totally satisfying end in itself.

 What do most people do on a date?

'Dates are for having fun. People should use them to get to know each other. Even boys have something to say, if you listen long enough.' *(Lynnette, age 8)*

Obsession

The mark of an obsession is that you are so caught up with the object of your desire that every other area of your life is affected. A person in love finds it more difficult to concentrate on their work, to keep their personal affairs organised, to gain such high marks in their studies while their previously all-consuming hobbies lose their attraction. John recalls when he went away on holiday that he was surprised to find himself dreaming about Anne all day as he lay on the beach! At that stage he hadn't said a word to Anne about his growing fondness for her. On his return from holiday he couldn't keep quiet any longer

Anne who was a secondary school teacher at the time remembers having to discipline her thoughts during the school day so that she could concentrate on the lessons. Anne found a neat solution 'I carried a little photograph of John around with me, and I thought I could afford to think about him when I was doing stationery duty in the lunch hour. I would just have to wait for girls to arrive to ask for their books - I would give them out in a mechanical sort of way. Little did they know that in between the rough books and the neat books I was looking at the picture of my beloved and wallowing in the feelings that were overwhelming me!'

What is the right age to get married?

'Twenty-three is the best age because you know the person FOREVER by then'.
Camille, age 10

Illusion

The illusion of falling in love is that the person you love is perfect! Listen to anyone describing their new heart throb and you would think that they have just found the most good looking, intelligent, witty, kind, and sensitive person on earth! This perception is often devoid of objective reality. A failing university student can be described by his girlfriend as 'very intelligent', as she overlooks the fact that he is lazy, and didn't work for his exams. Susan described her new boyfriend as strong and protecting. Her friends' view of him was that he was dominating and controlling. Richard was overwhelmed by the beauty of his amour but overlooked the fact that she was neither interested in the same things as him, nor had the intellectual capacity to converse with him about those things.

The old adage 'love is blind' is based on watching people at this stage of falling in love. The discovery of 'irritating habits' is all in the future. If that discovery doesn't happen until after marriage it can be quite a disturbing shock.

Sexual arousal

Another mark of falling in love is the awakening of strong sexual desire. While for a woman this is often a general sense of physical pleasure, for a man this is more likely to be located in his genitals. There is an instinctive physical attraction which draws lovers together. There are two particular marks of this stage of the development of physical relationship.

16

One is that both man and woman have an aroused physical longing for each other and an impelling desire to proceed to the next stage of intimacy, concluding in sexual intercourse. Later in marriage it is frequently true that women in particular lose this longing, and are more often content simply to be hugged, rather than to have intercourse.

The force of this physical attraction can be so strong that even a Christian couple who want to remain celibate before marriage find it hard to resist. James and Tricia, both committed Christians, from Christian homes were surprised at the power of this attraction which proved overwhelming for them. Tricia became pregnant, at a time when James was wondering whether to end the relationship. They had 'gone further' than they had intended and now felt trapped and drawn into a marriage for the sake of the baby.

The second mark is that it is hard to imagine that you would ever be attracted to anyone else!

Self-pleasing

When we fall in love we feel we would give up anything to be with the beloved, and we would do anything for them. Although this may sound very altruistic it is often unknowingly driven by a self-centred motivation. In truth we want to be with them because it gives us such a good feeling.

John was a bachelor when he was ordained and Anne was a member of the church where he served his first curacy. While out on a walk one day with his sister he happily described his new love to her 'I think she is just right for me - if I married her my life would be really improved - it would be wonderful for her to come alongside me and for us to serve the Lord together - she will be a real asset to my ministry'. Her reply exposed this selfishness in him 'John how dare you think of just marrying someone to improve your life; marriage is not about what you get, it's about what you give to each other.'

> *A frog said to a fair maiden, 'I was once a handsome prince until an evil witch put a spell on me. One kiss from you and I turn back into a prince and then we can marry. We can move into the castle with my mum, you can prepare my meals, clean my clothes, bear my children and forever feel happy doing so.'*
> *That night the maiden had frog's legs for dinner!*

Most couples know what it is to fall in love. In the Western world we marry on the basis of this experience, and many people expect these feelings to continue such that they live 'happily ever after'. Of course it only takes a moment's thought to make one realise that this is unrealistic. The nation's work output would suffer from constant lack of concentration, at the very least! Some research has shown that the 'falling in love symptoms' last on average two years!

When a couple emerge from the euphoria of this 'in love phenomenon' they are at a very critical, but potentially enriching moment within their relationship because they can begin to discover the nature of true love. It may be quite a frightening moment because they begin to view each other with a greater objectivity, mixed with a greater capacity to criticise. 'You never put the seat down when you have used the loo' becomes a powerful and divisive accusation. 'You're never on time!' 'You're always staying late at work - we never spend time together any longer!' 'Why can't you ever put your dirty clothes in the wash basket?' 'We're overdrawn again - what on earth have you been shopping for now - I told you that we couldn't afford anything else!'

John remembers his first vicar talking with him about the early years of marriage. 'You will realise that although you thought you knew Anne well you didn't really know her at all. That may not surprise you. What will surprise you is that you will discover you never really knew yourself. And you will find out just how selfish you are!' His words proved true!

At this stage a couple are beginning to unearth their own true personal identity. The masks of illusion are being removed. They are then faced with a choice. Will they learn to love each other in a deeper way? Or will they grin and bear what they think is a loveless marriage for the rest of their life? Or will they abort this marriage and look for another one which gives them the same euphoria as this relationship originally did? Sadly this last is the choice that increasing numbers of people are taking. As someone once said 'The ideal becomes an ordeal so we look for a new deal.'

However changing a partner does not bring the emotional happiness or stability that it might purport to. In the USA today whereas 40% of first marriages end in divorce, sixty percent of second marriages, and 75% of third marriages end the same way.

True love is a choice

The deception is that true love is based on feelings alone. God's true love for us is not based on feelings. His love involved a costly choice 'For God so loved the world that he gave his one and only Son, that whoever believes in him shall not perish but have eternal life '(John 3:16). For us too true love involves a choice. It is the same choice to give that God made. His choice was to give up his Son for us. Our choice is give up our self-centredness for the sake of our marriage partner. It is to give up what I want in favour of what my spouse wants.

The realisation of the fact that love involves a choice and is not just a feeling is potentially an enriching and defining moment within a marriage. It is what moves the marriage from something which each is 'using', albeit subconsciously, to bring them satisfaction, to a God-given friendship in which two people can commit themselves to enabling each other to become more like Jesus.

Every Christian is called to encourage and enable others to draw closer to Jesus. It is a call that transcends all natural barriers. 'To love our neighbour as ourselves' is meant to include our enemies, (Matt 5:44 love your enemies), those that persecute us (Bless those who persecute you Rom:12.14), and those of other races, (the parable of the good Samaritan Luke 10); and so it certainly includes one's spouse!

To make the choice to love one's spouse is no different from choosing to love any of these types of people. Whether we 'feel' we are in love or not we still need to make the choice to love. People who still feel in love may not see the need to make this choice, because their feelings are potentially blinding them to the true nature of love. People who no longer feel in love may not realise the power of choosing to love. The consequence of making this decision to love one's spouse leads to the experience of being truly in love.

Robert and Catherine, married for two years, recently spoke to us. 'We are more in love now than ever.' said Catherine. 'He still loves me when I am horrible'. She didn't think Robert had seen that side of her character before they got married. Its not that she was or has become a horrible person. She is aware of her faults, and was afraid that they would distance her from her husband. In these circumstances some will try to hide themselves further from their partners; others will excuse their faults and blame their partner. She has become willing to be vulnerable and to admit her faults; his understanding of unconditional love enables her to be secure enough to admit to her failings, and seek to change.

 *Talking point*

• *Recall together how you both fell in love.*
• *Remind yourselves of those madly 'in-love' moments at the start of your relationship.*
The recollection of having fallen in love is a powerful help in overlooking the faults in each other that may now have become the focal point of mutual criticism.

CHAPTER 2

Leaving the past

'We must go and see my parents this weekend' argued Dee. 'We haven't visited mine for months' retorted Richard, 'We haven't got time to see both, and we must get the bedroom redecoration finished this weekend.' 'Don't you care about my parents then?'

Dee and Richard found themselves in a recurring dilemma which frustrates many newly-married couples. They were trying to satisfy the expectations of both sets of parents, and at the same time satisfy their own personal desires for their marriage. This juggling act was proving as difficult for them as for many other couples.

The Bible recognises the possibility of a conflict of interest stemming from two different backgrounds when God sets the first married couple in the garden of Eden. 'For this reason a man will leave his father and mother and be united to his wife, and they will become one flesh'(Gen 2:24). It's interesting to note that God addresses these words to the first couple who were later to become the first parents. It was important for them to know from the start that their children would one day leave them in order to set up a new family unit.

When Jesus is asked about the possibility of divorce, which is usually the end result of unresolved conflict, he refers to this same passage. He is recognising the power of parental claims and the need for married children to be set free from their control in order to establish a new family. This leaving needs to happen emotionally as well as physically. Many parents still go through some sort of struggle with their newly married children to allow this to happen.

God is inviting Adam and Eve into a gloriously fulfilling relationship in which they will become increasingly united in heart, mind, body and spirit. For that to happen there needs to be a conscious act of will to leave behind an unthinking conformity to their background, and to find an agreed way of living out their hopes for marriage.

Becoming united

Establishing a new marriage takes time and commitment. God makes provision for this in the Old Testament where principles for family life are laid down so that couples can enjoy life to the full. 'If a man has recently married, he must not be sent to war or have any other duty laid on him. For one year he is to be free to stay at home and bring happiness to the wife he has married.' (Deut 24:5) In those days a wife's happiness was to a large degree dependent on her husband being physically present with her so that together they could talk and work out how to live life together. Obviously military service would take the newly wed husband away from home, and so God said he must not be made to do this.

In our society today it will probably not be military service that could separate a couple. It is more likely to be such things as an over-demanding job with the necessity of travelling away, time-consuming hobbies that only interests one of the couple, or for a Christian couple a demanding church ministry in which only one is involved. Some of the things which consume our time seem almost beyond our control, but others simply require a little forethought and self-discipline to manage better. A job comes into the first category, whereas a hobby comes into the second. Serving God together is one of the greatest privileges and blessings for any couple. In the early years of marriage there is a special value and enrichment that comes from engaging in hobbies and Christian Service together, and using one's home for hospitality.

In the example above what should Dee and Richard do? There are no inalienable God-given rules about how frequently they should visit each set of parents. Their dilemma is that they now have two sets of parents to visit, double the number of relatives and friends to stay in touch with as well as a new home to set up! There are still only 24 hours in the day and they will need to apportion their time carefully. Only when they have come to some agreement can they set about explaining their decisions and presenting a united front to their respective families.

This example highlights the fact that we bring into our marriages all sorts of hidden expectations from our backgrounds. This 'baggage' comes from a number of sources. The culture we have been brought up in, our childhood home, our beliefs about God, and any former marriage are all things which will influence the way we behave and the way we think married life should function. As you look at these you may find that you suddenly become aware of differences that you had not previously recognised or articulated. The husband and the wife bring two possibly very different, sets of expectations with them. You could say it's a sure fire recipe for disaster! The greater the difference in background, culture, and creed the more time will be needed to face the clashes when they occur. The successful resolution of them through patient discussion is a major step towards building a fulfilling marriage.

Factors Affecting Marriage

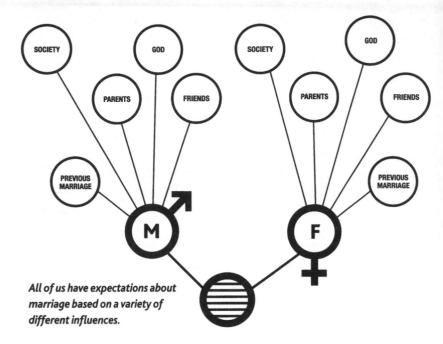

All of us have expectations about marriage based on a variety of different influences.

Our culture

In our church in North London, a very multi-cultural area, there are several mixed race marriages. God loves cultural diversity and so should we. But this diversity may result in a couple bringing widely differing expectations into their marriages based on their different cultural backgrounds. Most people grow up to assume that the practices of their culture are universally normal and correct. Sociologists talk about everyone having a 'world view'. Put simply; this is like a set of spectacles through which we see and interpret the world. Subconsciously we expect everyone to see things the same way we do. Take the example of time. In the West we live by digital watches, and time things down to the last minute. We expect the bus to arrive at 10.12 am when the timetable says it will. We are disappointed, even angry, when it arrives four minutes late! In Africa time is seen in a different light. Someone might wait for hours without rancour for the bus to come 'in the afternoon'. Each person behaves in a way that he/she believes is quite normal. It is our subconscious world views which determine what we define as normal.

Conflict arises when world views clash. Punctuality is one of the sources of arguments in many marriages. The potential for major conflict is increased between people with different world views on time. What may appear rather endearing in courtship, namely always being 'a little late' can become a major irritant when lived out on a day to day basis.

 Definition of a married man:

A person who has learned to turn off the car engine when his wife calls: 'I'm just coming!'

The fact that two people speak the same language or come from the same nation does not mean they will necessarily bring the same expectations to marriage. In our own nation of England there are significant differences of outlook between people brought up in different parts of the country, or in different socioeconomic groups.

One way in which parents have in the past tried to avoid the divisive impact such differences can have on a marriage is by arranging their children's marriage. This is still the practice in many parts of the world, and there is some evidence that the divorce rates amongst those whose marriages have been arranged is lower than amongst those who marry on the basis of falling in love.

Divorce

In the UK the expectations of people as they approach marriage today are quite different from those who were married 50 years ago. As a result of this it is now far easier to contemplate the possibility of divorce than ever before.

A vicar of a large church in the South of England said not long ago that he believed that nearly all the people at whose marriage he officiated harboured the secret thought 'If this doesn't work out in the next year I can get divorced and start again.' A new phrase has entered our language to allow for this changed mind set - serial monogamy. This now best describes the world view of marriage of many in our society. The belief is that 'I will be faithful to my partner while I am with her, but when the relationship is no longer satisfying to one or both of us then we are free to find another partner to whom we will be faithful for the next period of our lives.'

This radical change of outlook in our society has had a major impact on the views of Christians too. Though few would acknowledge they are consciously viewing divorce as a possible way out of a difficult marriage it is there subconsciously in the minds of many. The debate in the Church of England over the remarrying of divorcees in church is some indication of the way the church is responding to and even being moulded by the changes in society. If one person in a marriage embraces the possibility of divorce and if this is not identified and addressed, great fear and consequent destabilising patterns of relating can result.

Wealth

Another major change in expectations in our society is over actual or anticipated wealth. Many young couples, the majority of whom are already living together, postpone their marriage 'until they can afford it'. The cost of the average wedding in this country is now reckoned to be about £14,000. This places huge pressure on a couple to have a reception and honeymoon which are beyond their financial means. Additionally they might well expect to move into a house they own (admittedly with a heavy mortgage) and have it decorated 'just the way we want it.' These expectations are in stark contrast to that of a previous generation. For Anne's parents the desire to be married outweighed the desire for nice furnishings. Anne well remembers the wooden crate, originally a box for transporting oranges, in her parents' home which had served as a cupboard for baby, and then as a bedside table. The relative wealth, or spending power, of the partner's backgrounds may be the cause of other unexpected clashes.

Family background

Every couple, however diverse or similar their cultural background, brings unspoken and unconscious expectations from their family home into a marriage. It may be some time before they become apparent; many couples discover that the arrival of the first child brings these differences to the surface.

Differences of family background may become apparent over the importance and style of family celebrations; for the one they may not be particularly significant whereas for the partner they are a cause for endless preparation and expense! How to celebrate Christmas? how much to spend on birthday presents, what constitutes a Christening party? - these are all matters about which we make assumptions based on our own childhood family traditions.

Every new couple sets up a new home and brand new family. Over time they need to recognise and value each other's family traditions and lifestyle. Then they should carefully work out together what family traditions they want to establish and perpetuate in their own new family. They have to hold their childhood family traditions lightly so that they can be united with each other in forming new ones.

 What is marriage?

'Marriage is when you get to keep your girl and don't have to give her back to her parents' (Eric, age 6)

Our childhood home is also responsible for forming many of the beliefs, rational and irrational, that we acquire. If our parents had very firm views and opinions, they probably still do when we marry and they may try to influence the newly-marrieds too. The jokes about overpowerful in-laws may begin to look as if they have a basis in reality. The parents who have insisted on a daughter's weekly visit may still expect to see her as often along with her new husband. To return to the couple at the beginning of this chapter, they needed to face their own hidden doubts and fears about each other. 'Maybe he doesn't like my parents', 'Maybe she will not be willing to break away from them and it will be a continual pressure'. Only when they have faced these honestly, admitted to weaknesses and offered to help each other through them, can they go on to decide on the appropriate course of action for the given issue.

The marriage relationship that our parents modelled to us can also be a powerful determining force in our own eventual marriage. The man who has had a devoted mother who cared for his every need at home and kept a spotless house can unthinkingly expect his lovely new wife to do the same and hold down a full-time career as well! When we got married Anne moved into the curate's house that John had already been living in for the previous two years. He had not been noted for his tidiness during that time. However a few weeks after Anne moved in as wife, John was seen running a finger along the skirting board to check that there was no dust left there! Learning to laugh together in this situation is always a good way of defusing the potentially explosive indignation caused by this sort of unrealistic expectation.

Little girl to mother; 'Mummy do you and Daddy have sexual relations?'
Mother, caught off guard for a moment, managed a nonchalant admission without seeming too embarrassed 'Oh yes!' she said, congratulating herself on sounding so cool.
'Then why haven't I met any of them?' the little girl complained.

Siblings

The new couple may also need to sever strong ties to siblings. This is particularly true for twins or triplets who marry. The twin has to leave the close relationship with the other twin in order to cement the new relationship with the marriage partner. The partner who is not a twin can otherwise feel that there is an invisible third party in the marriage! A recent report from Relate listed 30 common things which can lead a marriage into trouble - it included both 'overpowerful in-laws' and 'marrying a twin or triplet'. The inference is that most people neither identify the power of their family backgrounds on their behaviour, nor talk through these things with their spouse adequately to gain the freedom to find a common mind.

Our view of God

Everyone brings into their marriage some degree of awareness of God. This may be a well-articulated faith, a childhood memory, an inarticulated spirituality, or an agnostic view of life. It may or may not include a pattern of church-going, and an expectation of what church life should be like. This affects the way people spend their leisure time, how they structure their social life, and what they commit their time, energy and money to. Generally the more deeply religious faith is held and the more definitely it is worked into a pattern of life, the more potential there is for a clash with a spouse who differs either in theological outlook or moral practice.

In the Old Testament God frequently reminds his people to marry only fellow-Jews - 'Do not intermarry with them' (non-Jews). 'Do not give your daughters to their sons or take their daughters for your sons' (Deut 7:3). One reason for this is that God wants his people to remain faithful to him; 'for they will turn your sons away from following me to serve other gods' (Deut 7:4). But another is a purely practical one; God understands the power of religious faith and the possibility of it either drawing people together or driving them apart. For the well-being of future generations 'do not give your daughters in marriage to their sons or take their daughters for your sons. Do not seek a treaty of friendship with them at any time, that you may be strong and eat the good things of the land and leave it to your children as an everlasting inheritance.' (Ezra 9:12)

In the New Testament this understanding is reinforced; 'do not be yoked together with unbelievers. For what do righteousness and wickedness have in common? Or what fellowship can light have with darkness? What harmony is there between Christ and Belial? What does a believer have in common with an unbeliever?' (2 Cor 6:14) Our God is full of compassion and because of that compassion he has made clear some of the potential points of conflict within marriage.

Even when firmly committed Christians marry they may have a differing or only half formed understanding of what God's intention for marriage is. An example might help here.

Right at the beginning of our marriage Anne had an image of how the ideal Christian wife should be submitted to her husband. She thought she should let John lead in everything while she followed meekly behind as it were. Further he should make all the major decisions and be the public spokesman for us as a couple. If John was the director Anne was to be the manager of the family firm. Anne says 'I knew that the Bible said in Ephesians 5 "Wives, submit to your husbands as to the Lord," and in an effort to fulfil this I tried to keep quiet and subordinate all my thoughts, wishes, and opinions. I kept this up for about six weeks by which time I was so miserable that John finally asked me what the problem was'. On hearing my tearful explanation and conclusion that I was a failure at being a good Christian wife John responded 'I married you because of who you are, with all your wisdom and experience. I don't want to be the one to carry all the decision-making - marriage means doing it together.' Talking over our new roles as marriage partners helped us to see where we were both coming from and how we could go forward together.

Our beliefs about what God requires, and who God is, can affect us powerfully, and those beliefs may or may not be grounded in bible teaching. If they have simply come from tradition or from wrong teaching we may need to leave them behind in order to be more fully united to our spouse. For example the tradition of the 'stay at home wife' may not be relevant in our society where girls are equally educated and our homes are furnished with labour-saving devices. The false idea that God punishes those who divorce can mean that a divorcee brings an unbearable burden of guilt into any second marriage. If a church does not teach that God is a merciful and forgiving Father, who welcomes those who repent and admit their failings, and sets them on their feet again by the power of his Holy Spirit, a divorcee may want to have nothing to do with God or his church since that association evokes such uncomfortable feelings.

We shall need to be open with our marriage partners about our beliefs and be prepared to find the right way forward together in leaving the past behind. Good communication before marriage and good marriage preparation will enable many to identify some of their differing beliefs and practices. But others may well emerge once a couple are living together day in day out. For instance, do you believe it right to say grace before every meal? Do you want to pray together, or read the Bible together every night? Who should tell Bible stories to the children? Should you make your children come to church with you? At what age do you let your children go to another church on their own 'because your church is boring'? Our family background will interact with our personal beliefs here. There is not necessarily a right and a wrong answer to these questions. What is important is that a couple are free to talk about them in an unheated way, discover their common mind, and be united in it.

 A Bishop once heard an evangelist telling this joke:

'I've spent many happy hours in the arms of another man's wife ... (dramatic pause) ... my mother's!'
The Bishop later tried to repeat the joke in the middle of a sermon. 'I've spent many happy hours in the arms of another man's wife ... (dramatic pause) ... but for the life of me I can't remember whose!'

A previous marriage

It is increasingly common for people to be in second marriages. Any experience of marriage is powerful and life-transforming.. When a marriage is dissolved it is common for a person to feel that they have 'lost part of themselves'. This shouldn't surprise us because God says that in marriage 'two become one'. Despite this feeling of loss a divorcee takes all sorts of memories into any new marriage they contract. Some of these will be deeply buried in their subconscious because they are associated with dashed hopes, hurtful words, and damaging attitudes. Often the more hurtful those images are, the deeper we bury them, so that the pain of them is masked. In a new marriage something may suddenly trigger the memory and the pain may surface. This can be quite an alarming experience for the new spouse. Neither may initially have any idea what has caused the emotional reaction. Unless the hurting partner is given time and space to articulate their pain a new cycle of unpredictable behaviour is set in motion.

For example a woman might marry a man who offers financial security but is a very private person who finds it difficult to share himself in conversation. She discovers he prefers to watch TV of an evening rather than talk to her. It is not long before the attractions of his possessions fade. Far from finding security she becomes ever more lonely in a loveless marriage and before long they may separate.

She then befriends a colleague from work with whom she finds it easy to talk in the pub after work. The friendship that she longed for, and that had been so lacking in her first marriage, propels her into a second marriage. This time she is determined to do things differently. The evenings are going to be spent in intimate conversation, not watching the box. She feels doubly cheated when her new husband arrives home after a day's work and is only fit to turn on the TV! He is taken aback by the strength of her opposition to what he regards as a perfectly acceptable way of relaxing after a busy day. Her hidden expectations of evening activity based on the negative experience of her first marriage conflict with his expectation that evenings are meant to be for unwinding while mindlessly channel hopping.

Unless they identify and start to talk about these hidden desires she will make something much bigger out of them than is necessary. It is easy for her to think 'this is how my first marriage began to flounder, and the same thing is happening again'. Instead of finding a way of making the new marriage work she is already contemplating the idea of it not working.

Expectations

A marriage counsellor explained 'The biggest killer for marriage is unrealistic expectations. Until spouses learn to change these expectations and develop an unconditional positive regard for their mates there can be a lot of friction'. We have found that most expectations for the future are based on experiences of the past. In everyone's background there are positive things to value as well of negative things to be aware of. Both of these can make a contribution to a rich marriage. Use this exercise to help you to appreciate those things, to help you identify your expectations, and to plan your future together.

 Talking point

• **What differences are there between the two of you in**

   a) *your childhood homes?*

   b) *the cultures you were brought up in?*

   c) *your religious backgrounds?*

• **What are your dreams and desires for the future of your marriage?**

CHAPTER 3

Celebrating differences

Anne discovered early in their relationship that John is a perfectionist and she is not. This is never more apparent than when redecorating a room. John fastidiously fills every small hole, and then applies all the right coats of primer, undercoat, and topcoat, checking every minute for any runs in the gloss paint. Anne would rather splash on the right top colour in an attempt to achieve a general effect in the quickest possible time. This was discovered on the very first attempt to decorate our kitchen. John's angry silence greeted Anne's 'success' in mixing white emulsion with the newly painted red woodwork to produce a general streaky pink effect on the walls! Since then it has been a test of love and patience for us to learn to redecorate side by side.

Apart from natural differences in character and temperament between any two people there are also profound differences between men and women. A New York psychiatrist says 'Men and women are fundamentally different. In that sense every marriage is a mixed marriage'. The extent of the difference is a surprising discovery to many in the early years of marriage.

This is a surprise because there is a prevailing belief in our society that men and women should always be treated equally, having the same rights and opportunities. This has led many into believing that man and woman are actually the same in their nature. While we agree wholeheartedly with equal opportunities the popularity of John Gray's book 'Men are from Mars and Women are from Venus' (Thorsons 1993) demonstrates that men and women instinctively know they are different and want to find out why.

In Romans15:7 we read 'Accept one another, then, just as Christ accepted you...' Acceptance of each other in marriage is a first and vital step towards loving each other. Our differences often bring us into conflict, and we can too readily want to deny those differences if we fail to understand and enjoy them. 'If only a woman were more like a man' is the immortal line in a song from the musical *My Fair Lady*.

A nervous bride was terrified that she would forget what to do in church on her great day. At the rehearsal the Vicar told her what to do. 'Process up the Aisle, Stop at the Altar, and Sing the hymn; then you'll relax and enjoy it.'
On the big day she arrived at church, quietly whispering three words 'Aisle Alter Hymn'.
Many brides have been vainly trying to do that ever since!

God created human beings different but complimentary - He made them in his image male and female. There is an obvious intention to have two different but complimentary expressions of his image, rather like two sides of the same coin. You can't have a coin with one side; there are always two sides, heads and tails. One side is not better than the other, more important than the other, or more valuable than the other. The value is the coin. Although societies have not always valued men and women equally God evidently does, - 'There is neither Jew nor Greek, slave nor free, male nor female, for you are all one in Christ Jesus.'(Gal 3: 28). Jesus was as willing to die for a woman as a man, for a slave as a free, for a Greek as a Jew. In the society of Paul's day Greeks, slaves, and women were all looked down on and undervalued. Paul is saying that Christians should recognise that everyone is of equal value to God. The value God has placed on us is the value of his son's lifeblood shed in our place on the cross. This value is the same for a woman in her womanhood as for a man in his manhood. If we view the text in this way and then deny the difference between men and women we are actually failing to value either one or the other in the way that God values them, and wants us to value them.

We believe that it is important to have an understanding of some of the primary differences we outline in this chapter. Inevitably these are generalisations. We don't want you to feel trapped by them.

Present day Analyses

There are many modern testing procedures which highlight the differences between the sexes. The Myers Briggs Type Indicator tested a large sample of several cultural groups and reached the following conclusions;

In decision making men tend to focus on the objective reason for taking an action; women are concerned about how the action will affect people.

Men reach their decisions through logical analysis; women make their's based on their internalised values.

Men find their greatest satisfaction in doing a job well, while women may find their major satisfaction in meeting people's needs.

God's character revealed

When God created men and women in His image He did so in order to reveal different aspects of His character in each. Some aspects of God's character are revealed through traits which we commonly associate with men, and some through traits more frequently associated with women.

If we take a look at Psalm 103 we see this in the following way;

'...his kingdom rules over all.' (v19) - God is powerful - Men are physically strong.

He '...satisfies your desires with good things so that your youth is renewed like the eagle's.' (v.5) - God provides for his people - Men are instinctive providers.

He '...redeems your life form the pit' (v 4) - God protects his people - Men are naturally protective.

A mother was walking along the pavement one day with her young son explaining to him how men used to walk nearest the road so that they could protect their womenfolk from mud thrown up by the carriages going past. 'That's why Daddy walks on the outside and I really like that.' Now a couple of years later she notices that when she is with her son he always walks on the outside of the pavement. Why is it? It's because something in him is saying 'I'm becoming a man and I want to protect my mother.'

'...from everlasting to everlasting'(v.17) - God has an the eternal perspective - Men characteristically see the big picture.

'...the Lord's love is with their children's children'(v.17) - God is also interested in the detail - Women characteristically focus on the details of the picture.

(Even as we write this together this difference is apparent. John is constantly thinking of the broad outline of the chapter whereas Anne focuses on the details of the points.)

'Praise the LORD, all his works'(v.22) - God is a Creator - Women are creative and procreative.

'He made known his ways to Moses, his deeds to the people of Israel'(v.7) - God communicates with his people - Women are naturally communicative.

Women talk in order to process their thoughts and their problems, as well as to impart information. A newspaper reported recently that as many as half of all women contemplate suicide at some stage; yet the statistics show that more men by far actually commit suicide. It appears that women often manage to solve the problem by talking it through with someone. In contrast some men apparently keep things to themselves until such a point that the problem is so overwhelming and suicide is the only way out.

'The LORD is compassionate and gracious, slow to anger, abounding in love.'(v.8) - God is compassionate - Women are intuitively carers and comforters.

Saying good night to the children often means two different things to men and women. Because she is an intuitive comforter Anne sees this is as an intimate moment when the child has the chance to mention any difficulties at school or in the playground. She will make the time to console, hug and pray. John is more likely to pop his head round the door, make sure the lights are out, say a cheery 'Good night - I love you' and shut the door again before going out for his meeting.

These aspects of God's character may not be grouped in this way in every man or every woman. The balance in each of us varies. Neither a man nor a woman on their own fully reflect the character of God. When God says that in marriage 'the two become one' he is intending that in a healthy marriage all these aspects should be expressed. (In our view this is one of the reasons for resisting the pressure in our society to view the raising of children by one parent alone, or by two people of the same sex as equally valid as the traditional nuclear family.)

Because men and women reflect different aspects of God's character in marriage a couple have an incredible privilege to have another side of God's character opened up to them. But to do this they must be willing to value those differences and not minimise them. This valuing of difference is part of what Paul means when he writes 'Submit to one another out of reverence for Christ.' (Eph 5: 21) This is the first thing he says as he introduces the subject of Christian marriage. It is one of the foundations on which a strong marriage can be built. As a couple learn to value these differences they discover more of the character of God and the mystery of Christ's love for his church. Hence Paul concludes this passage in Ephesians with the words "This is a profound mystery - but I am talking about Christ and the church.' (v.32)

 'I'm lonely,' Adam told God in the Garden of Eden. 'I need to have someone around for company.'

'OK,' replied God. 'I'm going to give you the perfect woman. Beautiful, intelligent and gracious-she'll cook and clean for you and never say a cross word.'

'Sounds good,' Adam said. 'But what's she going to cost?'

'An arm and a leg.'

'That's pretty steep,' countered Adam. 'What can I get for just a rib?'

Sympathetic ear

When a wife pours out her troubles to her long suffering husband, he needs to understand that she is probably neither blaming him nor looking to him for the ultimate solution. She is simply looking for a sympathetic ear. John Gray, in his book 'Men are from Mars and Women are from Venus' (Thorsons 1993) recommends that a wife learns to tell her husband - 'It's not your fault'. He calls them 'four magic words'. Their magic is that they release him to listen without feeling he is being blamed or having to provide a solution; they also gain for her what she wants - a listening ear.

After a tense day at work Jan recounted to her husband Paul the problems of the day which centred around the souring of relationships in the office. He listened attentively and offered his advice. The next day she reiterated the story - nothing had changed. He re-offered his advice. When she mentioned the same problem for the third day running he was astonished and said to her 'I am not talking about this any further with you - you haven't taken my advice so far - there is no point in talking about it again.'

Jan was talking in order to process her own thoughts and feeling about the situation. Paul thought that he was required to solve the problem for her. All she was asking was that he would be a sympathetic listener. His failure to realise that led to them both feeling rejected when his unsolicited advice was not acted on.

Private space

John Gray also has four magic words for men 'I will be back'. He observes that men need space either to switch off from their responsibilities or to think on their own about how to handle them. He describes this behaviour as 'going into a cave'. If a wife can learn to allow her husband to do this she will probably be rewarded by his willing communication later. If she insists that he comes out of his cave, and talks immediately, it is more likely to drive him further into himself in the dark recesses of his cave. The magic words enable her to trust him to come back; they also gain him what he wants - some peace and quiet immediately, and remind him that he also has a deep need to communicate his thoughts with his God-given helper.

This difference is often exemplified when a couple return from work. When John comes home from a tense meeting he normally does not want to talk about it for a while. He may switch on the TV, walk round the garden, or hide behind a newspaper. Only later will he begin to verbalise his thoughts and feelings. In contrast, when Anne comes home she wants to spill it all out immediately over a nice cup of tea!

Differences between men and women

1. A woman has the last word in any argument. Anything a man says after that is the beginning of a new argument!
2. A woman marries a man expecting he will change, but he doesn't. A man marries a woman expecting that she won't change and she does.
3. A woman will dress up to go shopping, water the plants, answer the phone, read a book. A man will dress up for weddings and funerals.
4. Men wake up as good-looking as they went to bed. Women somehow deteriorate during the night.
5. A woman knows all about her children. She knows about dentist appointments and romances, best friends and favourite foods, and their secret fears, hopes and dreams. A man is vaguely aware of some short people living in the house.

Differing Needs

One of the consequences of our difference is that men and women marry looking for different things from their relationship. Some research recently carried out amongst 800 people on this issue came to the following conclusions which are listed below in order of priority

A man desires
Sexual Fulfilment
Recreational Companionship
An Attractive Spouse
Domestic Support
Admiration From His Wife

A woman desires
Affection
Conversation
Honesty and Openness
Financial Support
Family Commitment

Priorities and Needs

The first thing we notice when we look at these is that men and women come to marriage with very different priorities and needs. Until we come to recognise our spouse's needs, and begin to meet them, we will be married to a person who is constantly disappointed. That disappointment may not always be consciously felt or verbalised, but it will be there, just as the major part of an iceberg is hidden under the surface of the water. Frustrated desires can lead to emotional outbursts or unresolved arguments. Unless some understanding of these different needs is gained a marriage has a stormy outlook.

Sex

The first thing in the list highlights a different attitude to sex. Where a man is looking for sexual fulfilment, he's thinking primarily of the act of intercourse. In contrast a woman is looking for affection. Unless sex is in the context of affection it will probably be for her simply a mechanical act which she doesn't especially enjoy. Arguments over sex are some of the most long-running in any marriage. Different sexual needs are amongst the most frequently quoted reasons for the breakdown of relationship that are presented to marriage counsellors. Since this is one of the most foundational aspects of marriage we dedicate a whole chapter to it later in the book.

Recreation

A man is looking for someone to do things with him. In contrast a woman is looking for someone with whom she can talk openly, honestly and very personally. Men like activities, they like hobbies, they play sport, they fly, they garden, they white water raft. And they want someone to do it with them.

How do you spend a day off? This scenario is not uncommon. John enjoys pottering in the garden. Anne feels she needs to clear up the house and thinks 'I'm so glad that John is doing the gardening. When we are finished we can sit down and talk together'. But John wants Anne to come and do the garden with him. In the event John is thoroughly fed up because he feels his need of a recreational companion has not been met - instead of being together on their day off they have been apart. Its unlikely that Anne's need of conversational companionship is now going to be met with John in a bad mood. Moreover John's desire for a night of sexual enjoyment is less of a possibility because Anne has not had an evening of affectionate togetherness. Anne says that the solution came when she realised that her need of conversation could be met by her being willing to follow John around the garden with a small fork and trowel chatting as they went. John was then so happy that he was quite prepared to help in the house afterwards. You can imagine the rest!

Appearance

It may surprise some that a man is still looking for an attractive spouse. Some women hate the thought of dressing up for a man, they want to look attractive for their own sake, not for the sake of their husband. Other women, once they have married, lose the motivation of dressing to win their man, and as a consequence begin to put on weight and lose interest in their appearance. (Some men do the same!) Some Christian women even think it is unspiritual to spend time and money on personal appearance believing it right to concentrate on the mind and spirit. When a man marries he believes he is marrying the most beautiful woman in the world. He may want the impossible - namely that she stays as a twenty year old beauty! But he will be greatly appreciative of a wife who takes a pride in her appearance because it pleases him. He needs to continue to compliment her on how good she looks. If he does this in public as well as in private she will thrive and blossom even further.

 How would you make a marriage work?

'Tell your wife that she looks pretty even if she looks like a truck' (Ricky aged 10)

Home life

When our parents' generation got married most women gave up work to run the household and raise the children. Today the expectation of most women is that they will have a career during their married life, and that their husbands will play an equal part in the running of the home. But many men still assume that in addition to her career a woman will still manage the household. And although he thinks he should help in the house he is still looking for a wife to take charge and look after him. - He would like someone to wash his clothes, iron his shirts, and cook his food. A husband will probably expect his wife to know where his socks have gone when he can't find them in his drawer! In practise a woman often ends up both having a career and taking responsibility for the smooth running of the household.

Admiration

Everyone thrives on the admiration of others. Parents know the value of commending their children - without it they wither, and with it they grow in confidence and security. Adults are no different. When you agreed to marry you were expressing your undying admiration. That admiration had probably grown over a period of time as you had begun to notice something special in each other. Admiration is often based on respect. Often in our society this respect is gained in the context of some shared activity, or job. After marriage if that activity is no longer shared, which is often the case after children arrive, the opportunity for respect and consequent admiration decreases. Instead of a man hearing his working partner say 'well done' he now hears her saying 'why don't you ever come home early - you are never here when the children need you.' Her admiration has turned to nagging. The danger is that he might gain his affirmation from someone else in the office who admires his work.

Family Commitment

There is a deep longing in most women to have children. Allied to this is the desire that they will be properly fathered. Many a woman has made the decision to marry because she senses that 'this man will make a good father to my children.' On the other hand because of the poor parenting from their own fathers, some women are now opting to have children out of wedlock, and raise them on their own, for fear of how they might be abused by a father. However the ideal husband for most women is the one who will give time to his family and play an equal part with her in caring for their children. Ideally she will want him to play with them when they are small, take an interest in their health and schooling, talk with them about their plans for the future, encourage them to achieve their potential, and give a healthy male role model, especially for sons.

Meeting Needs

Why do I need to understand that my spouse's needs are different from my own? A person knows they are really loved when they are appreciated for what they are without criticism. So a man knows he is loved by his wife if his legitimate needs are met by her. And likewise a woman.

Love never makes demands. So don't exploit your knowledge of these differences to insist that your spouse meets your needs, or to blame him/her for not meeting yours. Use them instead to think how you can express your love more appropriately.

Understanding these basic differences between men and women enables us to express love in a much deeper way.

On the next page is a list of needs for you to work through.

Celebrating Differences

Work through the following list of needs putting them in order of highest need (1) to lowest need (20). If the husband fills this in first and then covers his answers the wife can then make her own list. Then compare your lists! Look carefully at your spouse's list and consider how you could help him/her to have their greatest needs met; this is true loving.

I need	Wife	Husband
to spend more time with the children		
to talk openly and honestly		
to hear you say you love me		
to know you are proud of me		
to spend more time alone with you		
to make love more often		
to know that you accept me as I am		
to know you find me attractive		
to make decisions together		
to live in better accommodation		
to be alone sometimes		
to spend more time with friends		
to have financial security		
to develop my career		
to pray together		
to have a tidier home		
to have more exercise		
to know our children are your priority		
to develop my interests/hobbies		
to have more laughter in our home		

CHAPTER 4

Recognising Roles

Douglas and Irene were driving together with friends to a previously unvisited destination. Irene was map reading, Douglas was at the wheel. 'Douglas I think we should have turned off there' said Irene. 'No dear - this is the right road.' After five minutes Irene tried again 'I'm sure we should have turned off'. 'No dear - I know this is the right road. 'Five minutes later Irene tried again 'We are on the wrong road'. 'Woman know your place!' retorted Douglas. After another five minutes Douglas turned the car round and silently and without apology started to retrace their route to the turning his wife had originally suggested.

Getting lost on a journey is often a bone of contention between husbands and wives. But Douglas' response was somewhat more severe than that of most husbands. It also reveals an underlying attitude he held of the role of men and women in marriage. He clearly believed that 'man is the head of the household' and that he should therefore be unquestioningly obeyed in all things. This attitude is typical of many brought up with a particular model of marriage practised by those of his generation. It is reinforced for him by a Christianity which has majored on the Biblical injunction 'Wives, submit to your husbands as to the Lord.' (Eph 5:22). While we believe that the word submit is one of the most important words used to describe how men and women should relate to each other, we think the quotation of that verse to justify Douglas's attitude would be quite a wrong use of Scripture. More of that later.

Here we want to explore the different models of marriage that people subconsciously have in their minds, and which determine the way they then live out their marriage relationship. From the earliest years of our childhood we observe the way our parents conduct their marriage; a model of marriage begins to form in our minds from then on. We observe other models and ways of relating as we see the marriages of friends, or as we watch TV soaps, programmes and plays. Sometimes these have a powerful positive influence on us 'I'd like a marriage like that'. Sometimes the opposite is true 'I don't want to be treated like that'. Gradually an expectation of roles is formed within each individual. Only if your marriage partner has an exact duplicate of your view will conflict be avoided. Because our society is changing so rapidly, and we are exposed to so many different models of marriage, the chances of that are so slim that it is important to explore this issue of models and role expectation further.

A Traditional model

The second half of the 20th Century saw a huge change in the focus of marriage for most people living in the Western world. Fifty years ago a man was the primary provider, continuing the primitive role of hunter, while his wife stayed at home raising the children. In this model the husband was seen as the leader, and the wife therefore as a follower. In his role as leader the husband exercised his authority either by taking all the decisions himself, or by abdicating domestic decisions entirely to his wife. In the family hierarchy the husband was seen as superior, and the wife as inferior. For this reason meaningful and intimate conversation was difficult.

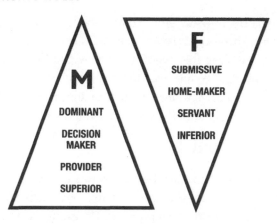

The following is an extract from a 1950's high school home economics text book entitled 'How to be a good wife'

'Have dinner ready. Plan ahead, even the night before to have a delicious meal on the table. This is a way of letting him know that you've been thinking about him and are concerned about his needs. Most men are hungry when they come home and the prospect of a good meal is part of the warm welcome needed.

Prepare the children. Take a few minutes to wash the children's hands and faces (if they are small, comb their hair, and if necessary change their clothes.) They are little treasures and he would like to see them playing the part.

Some don'ts. Don't greet him with problems and complaints. Don't complain if he is late for dinner. Count this as minor compared to what he might have gone through that day. Make him comfortable. Have him lean back in a comfortable chair, or suggest that he lie down in the bedroom.

Make the evening his. Never complain if he does not take you out to dinner, or to other pleasant entertainment. Instead try to understand his world of strain and pressure, his need to unwind and relax.

The goal. Try to make your home a place of peace and order where your husband can relax in body mind and spirit.'

Some men reading this might feel they would like to have been born 50 years ago! While we might all find these instructions amusing most modern women would be incensed by what they would see as exploitation of woman on a grand scale.

Partnership Model

This is the prevalent model today. In this type of marriage it is expected that both spouses earn a living, very often maintaining financial control over their own purses. Decisions are agreed upon mutually, and tasks assigned based on individual talents and abilities. For example the wife might be good at figures so she will do the household accounts (traditionally the husband's role) and the husband might do the cooking (traditionally the wife's role). Moreover the individual's rights are paramount and both are striving for significance and power in equal measure. If he has a night out a week, then she has the right to her night out; if she has to get up to feed the baby one night, then he has to the next. Neither is the leader and superior since they are partners. The husband can easily feel threatened and inadequate and a wife can fear that she might be taken advantage of. Consequently there is often a degree of competitiveness as each tries to prove their value to the other. Intimate communication may be blocked by this competition and so a couple can revert to living as so called 'married singles' each pursuing their own career development and personal interests.

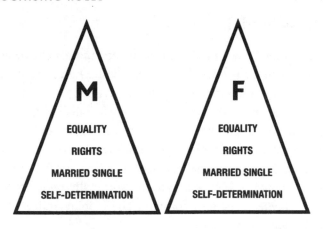

Both the Partnership and the Traditional models can work well. You probably know couples who subconsciously or consciously base their marriage on one or the other. Provided that both partners are happy with this, and the marriage remains functional, the marriage has a good chance of success. Christians may produce biblical justification for both these models. Those who support the Traditional Model will quote 'Wives, submit to your husbands as to the Lord.'(Eph 5:22). Those who support the Partnership Model will quote 'There is neither Jew nor Greek, slave nor free, male nor female, for you are all one in Christ Jesus.'(Gal 3:28) However we feel that neither fully captures what God intends for husband and wives.

When Adam stayed out very late for a few nights Eve became upset and suspicious. 'You're running around with other women,' she accused.
'You're being unreasonable.' Adam responded. 'You're the only woman on earth.'
The quarrel continued until Adam fell asleep, only to be awakened by someone poking him in the chest. It was Eve.
'What do you think you're doing?' Adam demanded.
'Counting your ribs.' said Eve.

Oneness Model

'For this reason a man will leave his father and mother and be united to his wife, and the two will become one flesh.'(Eph 5: 31)

At the heart of this model is a willingness to grow towards each other as God intended. There is a moment when a marriage is contracted; most couples remember the thrill of that first pronouncement from the officiating minister 'I declare that you are husband and wife.' As the marriage is consummated they are physically united as well as legally and spiritually united together. But God's invitation is to a constantly developing and deepening unity; the two will become one.

Unity speaks of harmony rather than domination. There is no place for superiority or inferiority as in the traditional model. It also speaks of integration; husband and wife maintain their individuality but are blended together to become one. There is no place for the competition so often evident in the partnership model which acts as a wedge driving people apart.

Patrick wrote to us after 13 years of marriage, which he admitted had sometimes been volatile because of the different expectations they had both come to marriage with. His wife had had an anti-male mind set as a result of a previous abusive relationship. He himself had had strong teaching in his church about the husband being the dominant head of the home and flared up in frightening anger when questioned. They both needed God's healing in their lives and he realised 'No longer can I take scripture and bash my wife with it - or point out where she needs to change. Even done in love I found my own interests tended to be served.'

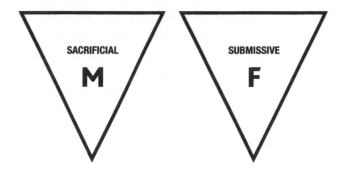

While there is considerable pressure from society to adopt one of the other two models of marriage there will probably be little pressure to adopt this one, because it is so significantly different and calls for a giving attitude on both sides. Most Christians know something of the pressure to conform to the morality and practise of the society in which they live. Paul wrote to the Christians in Rome 'Do not conform any longer to the pattern of this world,' (Rom12: 2) The way to resist such pressure is in the first place to gain a new understanding of what God wants - 'be transformed by the renewing of your mind.' This is as much true in marriage as in any other aspect of life. When we live life in the way God intends it we will always discover that it is the best way possible 'Then you will be able to test and approve what God's will is - his good, pleasing and perfect will.'

For a Christian the model for all our relationship is Jesus himself. His example was primarily one of servanthood. This was true even when he might have claimed to be in a position of authority - 'For even the Son of Man did not come to be served, but to serve' (Mark10: 45). As we follow Jesus we are gradually being changed by His Holy Spirit to become more like him. As we become more like him we will become more willing to listen, to serve and to encourage others. In marriage that means we no longer seek to dominate, or insist on our rights, but instead both husband and wife aim to honour and prefer their partner above themselves. It is not a case of 'give and take' but rather 'give and give'. Because this so goes against the grain of our fallen human nature, if we are to base our marriages on this model we must constantly be asking for and allowing the grace of God to be at work in our lives.

Mutual submission

The basis of this model is mutual respect and a willingness to submit to each other. Christians sometimes base their marriage relationship on Paul's words 'Wives, submit to your husbands as to the Lord' (Eph 5:22). A man, like Douglas in the opening example in this chapter, may wrongly use it to force submission from his wife. The first thing to say about submission is that it should be mutual. 'Submit to one another out of reverence for Christ.' (Eph.5.21). God does not ask anything more of a wife than he is asking of a husband. Lets look at this text more carefully.

Ephesians 5: 21-25

'Submit to one another out of reverence for Christ. Wives, submit to your husbands as to the Lord. For the husband is the head of the wife as Christ is the head of the church, his body, of which he is the Saviour. Now as the church submits to Christ, so also wives should submit to their husbands in everything. Husbands, love your wives, just as Christ loved the church and gave himself up for her...'

Wives, submit to your husbands as to the Lord.

A wife can choose to submit to her husband as she does to the Lord Jesus (v 22). Jesus Christ never forces us to give our lives to Him. He waits until we are so convinced of his love for us, because of his sacrifice on the cross, that we long to live our lives for Him. In the same way a husband should not force his wife to submit to his love. If he has to do that he is not loving her as Christ loves the church. It is up to her to choose to give herself to her husband, because she has come to trust his love for her. By choosing to put his wishes first she can love and cherish her husband. Her submission is thus a gift to him not an enforced obedience to a command.

What might this mean for her? It may mean that she will encourage him to go and play golf because she knows that he needs physical activity, switches off from the pressure of work on the golf course, and so he will avoid 'burn-out'. She might do this even though she would really like him to spend the time changing the washer on the bathroom tap! It may mean that she will joyfully make love to him even though she is tired and would rather go straight to sleep.

Husbands, love your wives

The way a husband submits to his wife is by loving her as Christ loved the church and gave himself up for her. (v.25) This is a tall order! Jesus Christ submitted his body to the cross for the sake of the church. How might this be an illustration of the love required from a husband? If a husband loves his wife more than his own body he will try, for example, to find out when she wants to make love rather than demanding it at his whim. He will consider his involvement in his sporting activities and try to discover how she would like him to spend his free time. He could encourage his wife to spend some time at her hobbies while he baby-sits. He could even make the choice to do something with her that he would not ordinarily choose to do.

John hates shopping so when he volunteers to push the weekly shopping trolley round the supermarket with Anne on his day-off, she really knows he loves her!

👁 *Do not marry someone that you know you can live with;*
Only marry someone that you cannot live without.

Divine restraint

Someone has said 'Man's power over woman is restrained by love. Woman's power over man is restrained by submission. The love of a woman and a man gains immeasurably when placed under this divine restraint.'

The truth is that a man could probably use physical force to get his own way. No-one witnessing such a thing would be impressed by the romance of the occasion! On the contrary it would be vile and repugnant. A woman can exercise power over a man through subtly manipulating him or using her sexual allure to arouse his desires and weaken his will. History is full of examples of men succumbing, against their better judgement, to a woman's wiles.

In order for a man and a woman to express real love to each other they need to choose to be restrained by sacrificial love and submission, and this is exactly what the apostle Paul is referring to in his letter to the Ephesians. Just as we are repelled by the sight of a man using force on a woman or the awareness of a woman manipulating a man for her own ends, we are attracted by the sight of a marriage bonded by sacrificial love which is under divine restraint.

When we were in New Zealand recently we visited the Huka Falls, and stood awe-struck watching the magnificent pounding waters of the Waikato river thundering through a narrow natural gorge. The swirling torrents with their deafening roar as they rage through the restricted channel hold a magnetic attraction for the tourist. By contrast, further upstream, where the river, unrestrained by a narrow gorge, flows lazily between marshy, muddy banks no visitors stop to admire the view.

For many in our society marriage has become a laughing stock or at best an irrelevance. It would seem that many in today's generation have seen little that would attract them to marriage. But we believe that as a couple work at their marriage it can become such a source of beauty, power and strength that we not only find hope for ourselves but also offer it to the next generation

---

 Talking points

Can you think of people you know who typify the three models of marriage outlined in this chapter?

Which marriages of your friends or family have impressed you and why?

In what ways do you see people submitting to each other in marriages of your peers?

Can you each think of a way in which you could willingly submit to each other to express your love?

On the next page is a checklist for you to work through together.

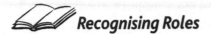 *Recognising Roles*

Work through this check list together and try to come to a common mind. Some of the issues that are identified are dealt with in more detail in later chapters.

	Agree	Disagree
The husband's career is more important than his wife's		
The wife should take time off work when the children are sick		
The husband should have one night out a week with his friends		
The wife should be responsible for shopping and cooking		
Husband and wife should take turns with the house cleaning		
The husband should initiate love making		
The husband should take the lead in spiritual matters		
Religion is the wife's responsibility		
The husband should do household repairs		
The wife has the greater responsibility for the household chores		
The wife is responsible for matters to do with the children's education		
The husband should take the financial decisions when the wife is not earning		
The wife should send birthday cards and presents to friends and family		
The wife should not query the husband's decisions		
The wife should plan holidays and the family social calendar		
The wife should organise baby-sitting		
The husband should baby-sit once a week so that the wife can go out		

CHAPTER 5

Communicating love

We were preparing to go on holiday. This had already proved to be a time of high stress in our marriage in the past. Anne's role normally was to pack the cases (no mean feat with four children) and to ensure the house was clean before leaving. John traditionally left everything to the last minute, and came home from work expecting to leave on the dot of the estimated time of departure. In tears Anne would frequently wonder whether holidays were really ever worth it. On this occasion Anne had to dash out to buy some last minute items. When she returned, fearful that John would be angry at their late departure, to her great astonishment she found John hoovering the hall. Her reaction startled him. 'Thank you - I never knew you loved me so much'. What was to him a simple practical act of preparation for their holiday was apparently for her an amazing expression of love. To his greater astonishment she kept telling the story to others all that summer!

John was discovering that love is communicated in more than words. He had until then been unaware of the powerful impact of what he viewed as a fairly insignificant event. He could express his love to Anne in a really convincing way through a simple small task such as hoovering, or helping her with a job she would normally do herself.

I love you

Our marriages will grow as we continue to communicate our love for one another. The words 'I love you' are important and need to be said often. If they are just said in a routine manner in the same way at the same time every day they can lose some of their power. A man who says 'I love you' each morning as he leaves for work is doing something precious, but the same words will have added value if he says them to her at a time when she is not expecting them. To whisper them in your spouse's ear as you watch your son playing football at school, or as you walk hand in hand to the shops, will communicate so much more effectively. Never underestimate the element of surprise.

We live today in a pressured society where time is at a premium. Many couples struggle to find and spend quality time together. Their busy work lives keep them apart during the day, and either their own, or their children's, hectic social or church calendars keep them apart in the evening. They may easily complain 'we never have time to express our love for each other.' Technically this may be true but to say 'I love you' takes barely a second, and can communicate so much.

If the words 'I love you' are only uttered by a husband as a prelude or invitation to having sex they have simply become a ticket to buy something that he wants. They have lost their meaning as a gift. When used properly they convey affirmation, cherishing, comfort and protection. When anyone receives that sort of gift their sense of well-being and worth is enhanced. In marriage we have the privilege of giving that gift to our spouse. When a couple learn to do this they build each other up in love, in a way that truly fulfils the Biblical exhortation 'Therefore encourage one another and build each other up,' (1Thess 5:11)

A couple went to a marriage counsellor after many years of married life. 'He never says he loves me' complained the wife. 'Is that true?' asked the counsellor. 'Yes it is - I told her I loved her when I asked her to marry me. I haven't changed my mind since, so I don't see the need to repeat myself!'

More than words

John discovered another way of communicating 'I love you' by hoovering the hall. It probably would not have been such a powerful statement on any another occasion. It was effective because Anne was not expecting it, and because she knew that it was not a high priority for him. John wouldn't have minded leaving the hall un-hoovered - after all they were going on holiday and no-one would see it for two weeks! He knew however that she liked to leave the house clean and tidy. The only reason he was doing it was to please her. She obviously realised this and was overwhelmed by this expression of love at a time when she would normally have been overwhelmed by feelings of panic.

This story not only points to the need to convey love in more than just words. It highlights the fact that for the message 'I love you' to be effectively communicated it has to be both transmitted and received in a language that is understood by both partners. Gary Chapman in his book 'The Five Love Languages' (Northfield Publishing USA 1992) examines the way people communicate love. He talks helpfully about different ways of communicating love as being the equivalent of speaking different languages. Everyone has a mother tongue. It is the language they both prefer to speak and find it easiest to understand. If someone starts saying something to them in a foreign language they may not understand even the simplest of messages, .and they will need to learn the new language in order to understand and be understood.

65

Chapman maintains that in the same way that people have a mother tongue for general communication they have a preferred language for communicating love. This is something that is as much part of them, their character, and their make-up as is their language. He identifies five most frequently used languages. As you read try to identify your own preferred, or primary, love language, and also try to identify that of your spouse.

 'I just learned how my wife ticks, when she began to tock!' Ogden Nash

Words of affirmation

The spoken word has great power. Some of us have experienced this negatively. 'You are plain stupid' is a phrase that has stuck in the memory of many a child. The power of negative words has been well documented. Research shows that if a parent says once to their child 'you are hopeless' at the beginning of the day a teacher will need to commend that child nine times before he will believe he is not hopeless, and begin to take pride in his work again.

It is not only children for whom affirmation is vital. We all need someone to believe in us and to express it regularly and frequently to us if we are not to believe the negative things that we all receive in the course of life. A married person has the opportunity and privilege of doing that with their spouse. The problem is that because of our familiarity with each other we often feel we have permission to point out each other's faults. More than that we take each other for granted and can neglect to thank each other for things that we would spontaneously and courteously express gratitude to anyone else for.

Anne remembers an evening meeting for newcomers in the Vicarage. At coffee time she brought in a chocolate cake she had made. John expressed his delight and surprise and immediately thanked her. A young man got up and left the room. Anne followed him to the kitchen to see if he was all right. She found him muttering 'I've never seen that before'. His explanation for his behaviour was that he had never heard a husband thank his wife for anything before!

 'I can live for two months on a good compliment' Mark Twain

A couple we know made a deal that they would never criticise each other in public. They have kept it for the last 30 years, and their marriage shows the benefits. A step on from this is to be able to compliment each other in public as well as privately. It is difficult to do it publicly if you don't do it privately so we all need to learn the art of doing it at home. Once learnt there it comes naturally elsewhere.

One Sunday John was saying goodbye to people at the church door having inadvertently left his radio microphone on. As a result the church heard him praise his wife for all the hard work she had done to get them ready to go to the New Wine Summer Conference. Anne felt very cherished!

Another way we speak words of affirmation is through the encouragement of each other's gifts and talents. It is surprising how many of us underestimate our ability or our achievements. It normally takes someone else to see what we are good at. As we take the trouble to commend each other we enhance each other's sense of value and well being. This often communicates love as much as the words 'I love you'.

Quality Time

Quality time is time given primarily to one's partner. It may be time spent in a joint activity, talking over a common concern, or planning something you are both involved in. It does not mean being in the same room, but engaged in different activities. Nor does it mean being together but conversing with other friends, for example at the same party. Nor does it mean one talking while the other is trying to read the newspaper or watch a programme on TV.

It could be watching a TV programme and reflecting on it together. It may mean sitting on the sofa staring into each other's eyes, murmuring sweet nothings at odd intervals. However in these days when we are so pushed for time it is more likely to be doing some sort of job together. A routine chore can be transformed into a springboard for romantic togetherness.

As a couple we have struggled to raise a family, serve the Lord, and look after a large house. We frequently complained about not having enough time together. Even on a day off which might have been dedicated to spending time together John spent his time on DIY, and Anne would have to do the weekly shopping. A solution came not through neglecting those necessary activities, but when we realised we could do these things together, and double-use the time. Anne discovered that clearing out the garage could even be fun since she now saw it as an opportunity to be with her husband. John didn't complain so often of a headache whenever he went shopping - it was now an occasion to be with his wife, and whisper sweet nothings in her ear over the frozen food cabinets!

Having said this we find that it is quite important to try to have a regular evening when we are not doing anything else apart from giving each other our undivided attention. A weekend away, designed to get away from all the activities and pressures of everyday life, can be a marvellous way of giving quality time. .

One evening a man and his wife called another couple to see what they were doing. 'Oh,' said the other wife, 'we're just drinking coffee and talking.' As she hung up the phone, she demanded, 'Why don't we ever do that? They're just drinking coffee and talking.' Her husband said, 'So make a pot of coffee.' They sat with their freshly brewed coffee, just staring at each other in silence. 'Well, call them back,' he directed, 'and find out what they're talking about..'

Receiving Gifts

We are not talking about extravagant presents here, but rather the little love tokens that may only cost a few pence, but say 'you are special and I love you.' For some the single rose, the bar of chocolate, or home-made card can touch the heart in a way that is wholly disproportionate to the value of the gift. The value lies in the way the gift is received.

Richard told us that he had discovered he could melt his new wife's heart with flowers. However he had to steel himself not to buy a pot-plant which looked better value to him since it would stay alive longer. She preferred cut flowers. He was a wise man. Instead of investing in a longer lasting plant he invested in his wife's heart.

If we want to say 'I love you' to someone who speaks the language of receiving gifts we will have to by-pass the arguments in our head that it is all an unnecessary waste of money.

Katherine and Nigel came to us because their marriage was in desperate straits. She felt unloved and unappreciated. As she told her story she complained that her husband had only once remembered to give her a birthday present in all their years together. 'I never thought it was that important and we have always been strapped for cash' he reasoned. 'I didn't want you to spend a lot of money - I just wanted some indication that you remembered me and had gone to the trouble to buy something, even a card' she replied.

As he came to understand the importance of gifts to her, as a way of expressing love, he realised that he held a key to improving their marriage.

Acts of Kindness

Gary Chapman calls these acts of service. Acts of kindness are the things that we do for each other in order to say 'I love you'. They may be so little that they appear trivial but they actually mean a lot to the person for whom they are done. Jesus was expressing love when he washed the disciples' feet.. The washing of feet was a normal practice in Palestine. But it was the host who would arrange to do this task and Jesus was a guest like the disciples. Why did Jesus do it?

John, who was amongst those who had their feet washed by Jesus, introduces the story with these words 'Having loved his own who were in the world, he now showed them the full extent of his love' (John 13:1).

When we think of how God has demonstrated his love for us we normally turn our eyes to the supreme self-sacrifice of Jesus on the cross. 'This is love: not that we loved God, but that he loved us and sent his Son as an atoning sacrifice for our sins.' (I John 4:10). But God has expressed that love in other ways too, including this act of service where Jesus washes the disciples' feet.

In most households the jobs are divided up so that we each have our roles; he takes out the rubbish and she put out the cat; he fills the dishwasher and she empties it etc. Does that show that we love each other? It may do. But it will certainly do so if it is a job that we do not usually do.

One of John's jobs is the family finances. It's been necessary to keep quite a tight rein on expenditure over the years - four children are expensive to bring up! Book-keeping is prolonged because of the number of invoices and the fact that his dislike of the job means he doesn't do it very often. On one occasion, as John's heart sank at the sight of these invoices and the hours of book-keeping ahead, he discovered that Anne had already gone through the pile of bills assigning them to the right accounts. He heard her saying 'I love you' through that unsolicited act of kindness and service.

Physical Touch

There are many ways we can touch our spouse to communicate love apart from the obvious physical contact associated with the act of sexual intercourse. But often, in the hustle and bustle of our lives, we neglect the hug, the holding of hands, the quick kiss and cuddle, or the shoulder massage that says 'I love you'.

Different ways of touching require different responses. Some physical touch takes only a few seconds and makes no demands on us - for instance a momentary brushing of bodies as you pass. Another touch invites our attention - a kiss on the back of the neck may be an invitation to turn and kiss with the mouth. Another touch arouses our passions and is all-consuming. All of these touches can convey love and are important for us all.

We neglect any of these at our peril. Most couples know the value of sexual intercourse. As the Church of England Marriage Service explains 'It strengthens the union of our hearts and lives'. There is a whole chapter devoted to this subject later on in the book. But many fail to understand the significance of other types of touch, which are not an invitation or precursor to further love-making. They are simply a way of saying 'I love you', in and of themselves. They are also one of the ways through which we are satisfied emotionally. They are the moments that for many of us keep the romance of our love relationship alive. Without them we starve. More than that the act of making love can seem like a sterile experience for one who has felt unloved and unnoticed because there has been no physical contact in hugs and touches through the rest of the day.

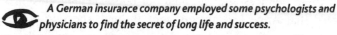 *A German insurance company employed some psychologists and physicians to find the secret of long life and success.*
Conclusion: Kiss your wife every morning before you leave for work!
Those who do
- *have fewer car accidents on their way to work*
- *miss less work because of illness*
- *achieve 20%-30% more than the non-kisser*

Mark was raised in a home where there has been little physical contact as a means of expressing love. Consequently he did not naturally hug his wife Kelly, frequently. Kelly had received a lot of hugging love as a child, and wanted to continue to receive love in that way. When she did not receive it she subconsciously felt unloved, even rejected. Mark was perplexed, even angry, when his acts of service around the house seemed to have little effect. The problem was that Kelly's preferred language was physical touch. Only when he learned to speak that language did Kelly begin to feel that she really was loved.

Learning to speak the preferred love language of your spouse is vital if we are successfully to communicate 'I love you.' Gary Chapman maintains that we all have one preferred love language in the same way that we all have one natural mother tongue. (We think that there may be many who are either bilingual, or multi-lingual.) It is important for us to discover both our own primary language, and that of our spouse, because they may be different. If we don't do this then despite our best efforts to communicate love the message may not be getting through.

Imagine a woman whose primary language is physical touch. If her husband is talking the language of acts of kindness, and enjoys bringing her breakfast in bed it may not succeed in communicating love. She is wanting hugs; he is giving toast and coffee. There is a communication breakdown!

We can fairly easily discover our own primary love language by looking at what we do naturally, almost subconsciously, in an attempt to say 'I love you'. What we give is usually what we want to receive. So the way to discover your spouse's primary language is by watching what she/he does naturally to you. Learning to speak another language requires a conscious act of will, effort, and time. In time it will begin to come more naturally, but initially it will require determination and forethought.

'Be devoted to one another in brotherly love. Honour one another above yourselves.' (Rom 12:10).

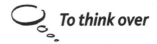 *To think over*

• *What do you do naturally to say 'I love you?'*

• *What does your spouse do naturally to say 'I love you'?*

• *When did you last do or say something in order to communicate 'I love you' to your spouse? What was it and how effective was it?*

• *How could you surprise your spouse by saying 'I love you' in their 'love language'?*

CHAPTER 6

Resolving Conflict

Jeremy and Elaine were driving back from a seminar on marriage enrichment. Tonight's subject was conflict. They had travelled there with great anticipation. 'I don't think there is much over which we are in conflict, is there?' Jeremy had said cheerfully on the way. The evening was about to reveal otherwise. One of the exercises they had been asked to do was complete a list of 'things I would like to talk about with my partner.' Elaine had ticked 'education of our children'. On the way home the discussion had started. 'I think we should do the best for our children don't you?' 'Of course' Jeremy replied. 'Then shouldn't we think about sending them to a private school' ventured Elaine, who as a teacher in one of the local schools had some idea about the educational system. That lit the blue touch paper for Jeremy. 'How on earth could we possibly afford that, on our salaries,' he retorted. 'You are always making suggestions like that without any idea of our financial position. We could never take on school fees as well as everything else.' 'But what could be more important than our children's future' replied Elaine rising to fight for the best for her children. And so it continued for the next 20 minutes until a stony silence fell while both of them internalised their anger and fear.

This example highlights a number of significant things which affect the way that couples get into conflict and then either resolve it or avoid it.

Communication is the key

Good communication is a bedrock for a good marriage. If a couple can learn the art of how to communicate in the different circumstances and conflicts of life they have every chance of working through the hiccups that any relationship goes through over a prolonged period of time. In contrast if a couple fail to learn how to talk openly and be vulnerable with each other they will probably find themselves growing further and further apart.

Conflict is inevitable

The director of the Tavistock Institute of Marital Studies, Christopher Clulow, maintains that if a marriage is to develop then conflict is inevitable. He observes that strong feelings of anger can surface at such times. 'There are times when you want your partner to get lost, but that's not terminal,' he says. A couple have a choice as to how they respond to conflict. By choosing to 'keep the peace' through not tackling a tough situation a couple can throw away what could be a chance to learn not only about their partner but about themselves too. 'If you take the exit route straight away you rob yourself of that opportunity and may repeat the pattern with someone else.' This likelihood is demonstrated by the fact that the divorce rate is higher amongst second marriages than first.

The way we handle conflict in marriage is key to the successful outcome or not of any given situation. Marital tension can be either creative or destructive. Michael Lawson, in his book entitled 'Conflict' (Christian Focus 1999), says 'marriage conflicts are opportunities for growth.' So, far from avoiding them or pretending (or indeed hoping!) that they don't exist we should be learning how to deal with them when they arise. Handled properly these times in our married life can bring us closer to each other. What we need is often a better understanding of communication.

 How can a stranger tell if two people are married?

You might have to guess based on whether they seem to be yelling at the same kids! (Derrick aged 9)

Good communication leads to true intimacy

Every couple probably longs for true intimacy in which there is a complete honesty and openness, and where inner thoughts and feelings can be shared without fear of rejection or ridicule. For this type of interpersonal communication to happen trust needs to be built between the two people. That happens as people climb the ladder of communication and reach the final rung

The five levels of communication

TOTAL HONESTY
AND OPENNESS

SHARING OF FEELINGS

SHARING OF OPINIONS

REPORTING OF FACTS

CLICHE
HOW ARE YOU? FINE? HOW ARE YOU?

Cliché

The base level of relationship is characterised by the simple question 'How are you?' This question doesn't demand anything from the person questioned. The anticipated answer is 'Fine' and at this level of relationship we are surprised if we get any other response. Indeed a disclosure of what a person is really feeling inside might be viewed as slightly shocking, stepping over the hidden boundaries of expected social chit-chat.

Facts

The second level is that of Reporting of Fact. Again this requires little effort or personal involvement. It is the normal way of beginning to explore areas of common experience or interest. 'How has your day been?' 'What did you do with the children today?' 'By the way, I've emptied the bin and bought some more milk.' These are all examples of day-to-day reporting of facts.

Opinion

The third level is that of Sharing of Opinions. It is characterised by the words 'I think that' at the start of a sentence. At this level a degree of self-disclosure is beginning as a person entrusts some of himself to another. Invariably men spend much of their time conversing with others at this level. Paul Tournier characterises the difference in the way that men and women use language like this. 'Women talk to express feelings and are more person orientated; men talk to express ideas and are more concept orientated.' Men are therefore beginning to find fulfilment for themselves as they relate and communicate at this level. As relationships develop most men fear that exposure of feelings will result in ridicule, and even rejection. The sharing of opinions only maintains a degree of security while trust continues to grow.

Feelings

The fourth level involves Sharing of Feelings. For this to happen, for men especially, a base of trust must have been built. Women, because of their use of language generally find it easier to develop relationships to this level of communication more quickly than men. They also feel less personally threatened by an expectation of having to share their feelings with others. Frequently in working with small groups we have found that in answer to a question 'how does that make you feel?' a woman will break the silence first! Men will sometimes say 'I feel.....' when they mean 'I think....' Feelings describe not how we evaluate a situation, but how it makes us feel inside our being. Feeling threatened, fearful, exploited, inadequate, sad, as well as feeling jubilant and happy, is something that we all need to learn to be sensitive about.

Honesty

The deepest level of communication involves Total Honesty and Openness. At this stage a couple have discovered the security that unconditional love can give, and in which self-disclosure without fear of rejection can flourish. Being able to voice one's deepest fears, and know that your loved one will not judge you or turn away from you, is the beginning of healing. It brings a level of intimacy and bonding that sets a marriage relationship on a firmer footing than before. But for many it will seem like an enormous risk and that is where trust comes in.

Building trust

So far we have talked about the development of a relationship through these different stages. However a couple needs to recognise the continuing importance of all these levels. It is not always possible to engage in deep meaningful conversations about self-image, identity crisis, or fears of failure at work. The demands of family life actually necessitate the reporting of facts as well. Many a couple has got into conflict because one has not reported back to the other, say for example about an important evening at school with a teacher concerning their child's education. And what man, wanting a little space when he returns home, would really want his wife immediately to tip out all her feelings about the day onto him? If he can't have space he can probably cope with facts, but letting it all hang out would be overwhelming. Knowing the time and place to engage in every level of communication is a skill that needs learning.

Let's follow an imaginary couple through the different stages of their conversation one evening on their return from work.

'How has your day been?' she asks.

'Fine,' he responds while reaching for a drink. 'What about yours?' (Cliché)

'Oh, not too bad, the department is being assessed next week.' (Reporting of facts)

'Do you think you're going to be ready for it?'

'Well we're really behind with a couple of projects and I don't know whether there's enough time to complete them,' she replies. (Sharing of opinions)

Later after supper, she asks him to clear up the dishes 'because I must look at some files for work'.

'I was hoping we could have a quiet evening in together, he complains, whereupon she starts to weep. What have I said now?'

'It's not you, it's work. I don't think I'm going to make it. I'm under so much pressure.' she sobs.

'You must be really worried,' he sympathises.

'The trouble is, I feel an absolute failure. I'm supposed to be efficient and in charge of this department, and I'm so afraid that we're not going to have everything ready on time.' (Sharing of feelings)

'Of course it will be alright, you're a brilliant administrator!'

Much later in bed, she confides,' I've always thought of myself as a second-best sort of person and that's why this job is such a pressure.' (Total honesty and openness)

Had he gone on to express his own fears for their marriage because they hardly ever see each other, or to express his worries that they would be in financial difficulty should she lose her job, one of two scenarios could have followed. Either they would have dived into a furious argument, or she would have withdrawn and they would never have got to the point of intimacy. Time and sensitivity to each other are both needed if conflict is to be avoided.

👁 *Often the difference between a successful marriage and a mediocre one is in leaving three or four things unsaid.*

Causes Of Conflict

1. Justifying minor irritations

Most of us are aware of the annoying habits of our spouses. We might even be aware of our own! But we tend to disregard these, believing that our partners' love should remain constant and rise above any such minor imperfections. However, toenail clippings left on the carpet, channel-hopping on TV, throwing dirty clothes on the floor rather than in the washing basket, can all escalate into major sources of frustration for the partner who has to endure them over a sustained period of time. If I choose to ignore my own bad habits, I may be the cause of increasing resentment in my spouse which could develop into a bigger crisis than I can imagine.

'Reframe' your reactions

It's a wise spouse who can learn to employ what we shall call the 'spin factor' to reinterpret annoying habits of his or her partner.. The wife who has heard her husband tell the same joke for the nineteenth time can save herself from being irritated by telling herself that he loves her enough to make her laugh! When he refuses to ask for directions on a car-trip she can reason that every outing is an adventure with him, so 'relax, put on your favourite music and enjoy it!' When she is map-reading and gets lost because she has muddled up left and right again, he can tell himself 'all the more time alone in the car to chat together'.

2. Innocent actions wrongly interpreted

Any problem can be exacerbated if the long-suffering partner wrongly concludes that there is a much more sinister and marriage-threatening reason for irritating behaviour. A tired husband who comes home very late may be seen by his wife as not caring about their marriage. He may be simply trying to keep his job by working the long hours demanded by his boss. But if he persists, after she has pointed it out to him, she may conclude that he cares more about his job than his family. An insecure, or unhappy, wife may easily fear that her husband may be 'seeing someone else'. Similarly a disorganised wife who can never be ready on time when they have arranged to do something together can be seen as not deeming her husband's concerns important. He may well come to think she does not care about him.

Man and woman

A man is a person who, if a woman says, 'Never mind, I'll do it myself,' lets her.

A woman is a person who, if she says to a man, ' Never mind, I'll do it myself,' and he lets her, gets mad.

A man is a person who, if a woman says to him, 'Never mind, I'll do it myself,' and he lets her and she gets mad, says, 'Now what are you mad about?'

A woman is a person who, if she says to a man, 'Never mind, I'll do it myself,' and he lets her and she gets mad, and he says, 'Now what are you mad about?' says 'If you don't know what I'm mad about, I'm certainly not going to tell you!'

Say it in love

We need to learn to give freedom to each other to express feelings of irritation and frustration. Unless we give time for this regularly the problem, though hidden, will be silently building up ready to explode on a later occasion. That freedom is a precious gift and we should not abuse it. A marriage counsellor warns: 'Married couples treat each other in a way they wouldn't dream of treating anyone else, saying very damaging things. Is that being intimate or taking advantage of a situation where, because you are bound together, you feel you can say anything?' She advises couples to treat each other as they would a good friend, to act with consideration, respect and love, and that means not saying or doing things at certain times.

We need to be courteously frank about our irritation with our partner's behaviour and the fears that it evokes, so that our spouse has the chance to reaffirm their love and commitment to the marriage by taking responsibility for their behaviour. The offending partner needs to admit to the need of breaking what is probably a bad habit. Where before, the particular action has not bothered anyone else, now it does bother a loved one and for that reason it must be addressed. If we persist in justifying our habits we show ourselves unwilling to love our spouse enough to try to change.

3. Big things unaddressed

Some issues are plainly more important. We will know from past conversations and experiences some of the major issues on which we differ. The way we deal with minor irritations can affect our willingness to look at these more major things. For instance if a man erupts with anger when his personal habits are questioned his wife will probably be afraid of expressing her feelings about his love-making. She will easily assume that if he is so sensitive on the subject of leaving the sink covered with shavings from his beard then he will be more explosive at any mention of his lack of foreplay when making love.

 **Exercise**

List in order of priority those subjects you would most like to talk about in greater depth with your spouse

- *Money/lack of/use of*
- *Sex*
- *Relating to in-laws*
- *Views of God*
- *Ministry of the Holy Spirit*
- *Praying together*
- *Size of family*
- *Children's future*
- *His free time*
- *Her free time*
- *Our home*
- *Interior decoration*
- *Holidays*
- *Unemployment*
- *Her career*
- *His career*

Be warned - this exercise may provoke conflict!

Reactions to Conflict

People react differently to conflict and it is important to discover and recognise both our own and our partner's normal response. Some typical responses are:

1. Blame shifting

'Its not my fault' is a common cry. In order to avoid uncomfortable feelings of guilt we frequently shift the blame onto someone else. In marriage that is normally our long-suffering spouse. Gillian Walton, Head of Training at the London Marriage Guidance Council says 'People have tended to blame others, like their parents, when something has gone wrong. There hasn't been great encouragement for people to take responsibility for themselves.' Generally speaking men tend to shift the blame.

2. Blame-taking

A mature person is able to take appropriate responsibility and admit faults. An immature, or insecure person is unable to distinguish appropriate and inappropriate blame taking. They will always feel in the wrong even if they are not. When one person in a marriage is like this they become the scapegoat for any marital conflict. Women are generally more prone to respond to conflict in this way than men.

If a blame-shifter is married to a blame-taker conflict may appear to have been resolved. In practise it has probably been buried in the blame-taker. That person will become increasingly unhappy in the marriage, and may not be able to put a finger on the reason.

If two blame-shifters are married then a stormy relationship is likely. Conflict will not be resolved until each learns to admit responsibility, to have the humility to say sorry, and to give and receive forgiveness.

If a marriage is made up of two blame-takers then these issues of conflict will result in increasing loss of self-esteem in both people. Silent unhappiness, and possibly hostility, will become the order of the day.

 Eve blamed Adam and Adam blamed the serpent and the serpent didn't have a leg to stand on!

---

3. Anger

Anger is often a mask for feelings of being powerless. In a marital argument it is used as an attempt to regain power when weakness has been exposed. When people sense they are losing an argument and don't want to admit they are wrong they may start shouting, become verbally abusive, and in the end physically violent. Men frequently react in this way.

4. Withdrawal

This is a defence mechanism against the difficulty of conflict. It may be an escape from emotional pain which surfaces as a result of conflict experienced earlier in life. For example a child who cowered helplessly in the presence of rowing parents might adopt the same reaction as an adult. The symptoms are silence, either refusing or being unable to contribute to the discussion, and sometimes the literal removal of oneself from the room. As a child they were helpless, but as an adult they can play their part in the discussion and help to bring the conflict to an end. An adult can be helped to adopt this new response by a loving spouse when given space and time. The process is hindered if the other partner remains angry and accusatory.

Resolving Conflict

1. Call a truce

It is not necessary, or always possible to resolve every conflict immediately. Besides that, passions are aroused in conflict which normally hinder any further rational discussion. In these cases it is important to recognise that there is a disagreement which is sufficiently large to necessitate further discussion. When anger has been evoked it must be dealt with quickly before it leads into sin. "In your anger do not sin:" 'Do not let the sun go down while you are still angry,' (Eph 4:26). Failing to call a truce allows anger to grow unrestrained.

2. Set a time

The couple in the car returning from the marriage seminar at the beginning of this chapter, needed to set a time to talk further. Given the pressure of life today, and especially for Christians who might be out of the house in the evening 'serving the Lord' the best way to deal with it is often to put a time to talk in the diary. This may not seem a romantic or spiritual way of resolving conflict - but we have observed that conflict between couples is rarely resolved by a simple 'let's kiss and make up' approach nor a 'let's do some spiritual warfare over this' solution. We have discovered that successful preplanned diaried discussions give the opportunity for the application of godly principles of forgiveness and reconciliation, and subsequently lead to an increase of romance! Not making an appointment prolongs feelings of resentment and allows bitterness to fester to the point of sin.

3. In private not public

'Not in front of the children' became a popular television comedy show. Everyone knows the wisdom of shielding our children from our marital disputes. However we need to ensure that they cannot hear raised voices after they have supposedly gone to bed ! We also need to refrain from drawing our friends or relatives in to our arguments. Dinner guests who are asked to take sides in what is obviously a point of conflict between the host couple will probably be too embarrassed to shed any helpful light on the situation. We have sometimes found it helpful to talk alone together over a problem while having a meal in a restaurant. Although it is a public place the setting helps to keep us talking and guards against 'flying off the handle'.

4. Reaffirm commitment

Many couples caught in the midst of an angry argument will think 'What has gone wrong with our marriage?' In truth nothing is intrinsically wrong with the marriage. Couples are bound to disagree at times because none of us is a clone of another. Something will only go wrong if the couple do not face the issue at hand. When talking about a sensitive issue we have found it helpful to say again that we love each other, and want to sort out the difficulty. Saying this may seem like stating the obvious under any other circumstances. But before revisiting an issue, which has previously caused an argument, those words can bring great reassurance. It can also help to hold hands as you talk, or to be within close enough proximity to each other so that you can give reassuring touches when necessary.

5. Deal with the issue not the person

There is a world of difference between saying 'I was upset when you were late' and saying 'you're never on time'. The first is an attempt to deal with a particular instance; the second is easily interpreted as a condemnation of the person's character. Try to keep the killer words 'always' and 'never' out of the discussion. 'You are always late and the food is always ruined' might lead the accused to jump to his own defence and cite a time he was not late. Justifying a lack of punctuality in this way will not lead to a successful conclusion to the discussion. To do this would also be failing to deal with the issue of 'feeling upset' which was the presenting problem.

6. Be willing to listen

Someone once said that listening is one of the greatest acts of love. When tempers flare all the principles we might have learnt about being a good listener seem to fly out of the window. Check yourself against this list of qualities in bad listeners, and try to avoid them when resolving conflict.

Bad listeners
- Interrupt
- Finish sentences for others
- Clock watch
- Answer the phone
- Provide quick or unrealistic solutions
- Rarely ask questions

7. Be willing to talk

Both partners need to be willing to express their thoughts and feelings. If one is not willing to talk it is impossible for discussion to continue! Sometimes a husband agrees to 'talk about things'. In practise what he means is that he will let his wife talk, while he appears to listen. He may be hoping that simply agreeing to the discussion will lead to resolution. Of course, in the process of talking what started out as a cool conversation can become quite heated! One partner (probably the woman) might be reduced to tears. Give yourselves time and try to maintain the willingness to talk again whenever it is possible to do so. Beware of using tears to manipulate the situation to one point of view.

8. Be willing to be the first to say sorry

A friend of ours, happily married for the second time, commented that many people enter a second marriage thinking, 'It wasn't my fault that the first one didn't work'. 'It's not my fault' is a common cry in our society generally - we seem to find it so hard to admit fault today and then apologise. There is never a perfect partner. Each of us needs to take responsibility for what we have contributed to the breakdown of any situation and be prepared to say sorry. It is vital to have made this decision to forgive right at the beginning of a marriage and at the beginning of any difficult discussion too. 'The creative way of handling tensions is to be prepared to forgive right from the beginning. This pledge of forgiveness lends great strength to marriage.'(Michael Lawson. Conflict. Christian Focus 1999).

9. Be prepared to forgive and forget

Forgiveness is a costly business because we often want to hold on to a grievance. Jesus pointed out in his story of the forgiven debtor, (Matt 18:23-35), that it is easier to forgive another's failing if you yourself are conscious of being forgiven forever by God. Since God freely gives us forgiveness we need to learn to freely give it to others - and who better than our spouse? More than that, God declares 'I am he who remembers your sins no more' (Isaiah 43:25). We too need to forget our partner's failings once they have been admitted and forgiven. That means not storing them up as ammunition for any future argument!

10. Be willing to get outside help

Some of the issues that cause tension seem insoluble. Some inevitably bring deep and uncomfortable feelings to the surface. In either of these cases it might be worth considering together going to someone else for wisdom. Many a newly-married couple, seeking advice from an older partnership, have been reassured that what they are going through is quite normal. In this case the help is informal, and the benefit of the older couple's experience is what is needed. Sometimes the help needed is beyond the scope of the average untrained couple. It may be that the point of tension is touching upon events in the past of one or other of the partners. An adult who has been abused physically or sexually and now faces difficulty in relating to their marriage partner can be helped towards healing through the wisdom and prayer of a trained counsellor or wise church leader. A couple who seek appropriate help for their ailing marriage, far from admitting defeat and failure, are committing themselves to building a stronger relationship which will be a joy to them and their children.

What about divorce?

The Bible clearly teaches that marriage is a covenant - a binding commitment which people should make with an understanding of its significance for themselves, and for society. In our society many view divorce as a legitimate means of resolving any irreconcilable conflict. Jesus seems to view divorce as an option only in cases of marital unfaithfulness. 'Moses permitted you to divorce your wives because your hearts were hard. But it was not this way from the beginning. I tell you that anyone who divorces his wife, except for marital unfaithfulness, and marries another woman commits adultery.' (Matt 19:8-9). In a large building there may well be a notice forbidding the use of the Fire Escape; but of course, if there is a fire, anyone endangered will use it. In the same way divorce is a legitimate escape route when the building of marriage is destroyed by marital infidelity.

Additionally Paul seems to teach that, when two people marry and one subsequently becomes a Christian, the basis of the original commitment has been changed. The unbelieving partner may use the occasion as a legitimate excuse for divorce, but the believer may not. 'If any brother has a wife who is not a believer and she is willing to live with him, he must not divorce her. And if a woman has a husband who is not a believer and he is willing to live with her, she must not divorce him. But if the unbeliever leaves, let him do so. A believing man or woman is not bound in such circumstances; God has called us to live in peace' (1 Cor 7:12,15)

The church has realised that there are extenuating circumstances in which divorce may be legitimately contemplated, and in these cases it is not a sin. It is right to get advice from a church authority on the subject.

We believe that the inevitable conflicts which occur in the normal course of married life can and should be resolved through patient discussion and prayer. The following checklist and Talking Points will help you to identify your responses to conflict, and improve your skills at resolving it.

 **Resolving Conflict**

Work through this checklist separately and then talk about the results together;

	Wife	Husband

I like talking with you

At the end of the day
On a day-off
At the weekend
Before going off to work

I find it easiest to talk

Sitting down face to face
Over a meal
Walking
While working on a joint project
In the car

When I feel criticised

I say things I don't mean
I withdraw into silence
I say things to hurt
I argue the point to prove I'm right

When I am grateful to you

I say thank you
I do something in return
I like to give a gift
I find it hard to express my gratitude

Talking points

- *On what occasions do you remember having a good talk? What factors contributed towards it?*

- *When do you feel closest to your partner?*

- *What makes it easy for you to share yourself?*

- *What conflict situations in your marriage can you remember?*

- *What was the source of the conflict and how did you try to resolve it?*

- *Can you identify your own and your partner's reactions to conflict?*

CHAPTER 7

Satisfying sex

'For this reason a man will leave his father and mother and be united to his wife and they will become one flesh.' (Gen 2:24).

For what reason we might ask? In the story of creation man is enjoying all the wonders of God's newly created world. All is open to his inquisitive mind - the wonders of astronomy, botany, and zoology beckon. Yet he is unsatisfied. Why? Because as the poet John Donne once wrote -'no man is an island entire of itself'. There is an inherent loneliness in being a human being that is only satisfied by relationship with another human being. 'The LORD God said, It is not good for the man to be alone. I will make a helper suitable for him.'(Gen 2:18) So God created woman. The Bible commentator Matthew Henry say 'She was not made out of his hand to rule over him, not out of his feet to be trampled upon by him, but out of his side to be equal with him, under his arm to be protected by him, and near his heart to be beloved.'

One of the ways man's inherent loneliness is comforted within marriage is through sexual intercourse. 'They will become one flesh.'(Gen 2:24) As a couple become one physically it is God's intention that 'through the joy of their bodily union they will strengthen the union of their hearts and lives' (as the Anglican Marriage Service puts it.) Sex is meant to be experienced within the context of marriage - 'man will leave his father and mother'. Good sex is normally experienced when a couple are really united, in harmony with each other - 'and be united to his wife'. And in turn it is also one of the means through which marriage is enriched. A good sex life will result in a general sense of well-being which can irradiate every area of life. The joy of sex is not just the joy of the moment, but also the joy that it releases into the rest of our relationship. Put positively when we have made love Anne will often say 'I feel closer to you now'. And for some reason this sense of being at one with herself and me affects other areas of her life too.

 A psychologist was giving a talk to married men about the need to make love regularly.

'How many here make love once every week?

A number of people put their hands up, looking contented.

'How many here make love once a month?'

A number of people put their hands up, looking less pleased.

'How many here make love three of four times a year?'

A very small number of people put their hands up, looking rather morose and sorry for themselves.

'How many here make love less often than that?'

One man put his hand up.

Do you mind if I ask how frequently?'

'Once a year' came the reply with a huge smile on the man's face.

'May I ask, then why are you looking so happy.'

'Tonight's the night!'

Songs of Songs

God never meant men and women to be prudish or embarrassed about sex within the marriage bond. As God describes Adam and Eve enjoying his creation he says 'The man and his wife were both naked, and they felt no shame.' (Gen 2:25) It was only their disobedience and fall that led them to feel shame about their nakedness in front of each other and so 'they sewed fig leaves together and made coverings for themselves'. Right at the centre of the Bible is the book The Songs of Songs. It eulogises the sexual relationship between men and women. Although it has rightly been expounded at times in Christian history to describe the intimate relationship between the Lord Jesus and his church it is primarily an erotic love poem. It is written as a series of love songs addressed to each other by lovers.

Sex is beautiful

The very first expressions from the lips of the woman evoke a longing for and enjoyment of sexual contact. 'Let him kiss me with the kisses of his mouth - for your love is more delightful than wine' (1:2).

Clearly full sexual intercourse is what the woman longs for 'Take me away with you - let us hurry! Let the king bring me into his chambers.' (1:4).

The man is not ashamed of or embarrassed by his sexual attraction to the woman. The provocative flash of her eyes, the way her hair bounces as she walks, the tantalising smile on her lips, and the sway of her breasts all contribute to his longing 'Your eyes behind your veil are doves. Your hair is like a flock of goats descending from Mount Gilead.' (4:1) 'Your lips are like a scarlet ribbon; your mouth is lovely.' (4:3) 'Your two breasts are like two fawns, like twin fawns of a gazelle that browse among the lilies.' (4:5).

Then a tender yet passionate kiss excites him further 'Your lips drop sweetness as the honeycomb, my bride; milk and honey are under your tongue' (4:11).

Yet she still hasn't given herself to him fully 'You are a garden locked up, my sister, my bride; you are a spring enclosed, a sealed fountain.' (4:12).

As he describes his desire in this way, and praises her for her beauty, she invites him to go further 'Let my lover come into his garden and taste its choice fruits.' (4:16).

Then with relief and excitement he expresses the joy of their sexual intercourse 'I have come into my garden, my sister, my bride; I have gathered my myrrh with my spice. I have eaten my honeycomb and my honey; I have drunk my wine and my milk.' (5:1).

They have aroused each other, and given themselves willingly to each other - they are satisfied in a way beyond any other sort of physical satisfaction that money can buy 'Solomon is welcome to his thousand coins, and the farmers to two hundred as their share; I have a vineyard of my own.' (8:12).

Sex in our society

The language used in this poem is tender and beautiful; though intimate nothing there seems crude or vulgar. In our society sex has been cheapened as it has become pursued relentlessly and indulged in almost mechanically. It has lost the alluring dimension of mystery. Writing in The Times (22 Mar 2000) about the future of Sex in the 21st Century, Irma Kurtz, agony aunt of Cosmopolitan magazine says, 'As we divorce sex from reproduction the motto will be "make money, not love." Sex will be an industry - and I don't just mean pornography. We will all approach sex as consumers. We will indulge our vices and sex will be just another little thrill. Its status will be like gambling, and while it is nice to have a little flutter, some people will become addicts.' We would say this attitude to sex comes not when it is divorced from reproduction, but when it is divorced from a stable loving marriage relationship.

In the same article the wonder and beautifying power of sex is expressed by Cambridge Philosopher John Forrester 'Sex embodies people's every day attempts to bring some sense of transcendental experience into their lives. In sex, through their partners and the acts they perform, people strive to give beauty to their lives.' God intended people to enjoy the wonder and beauty of sex within marriage. We believe that when it is rightly experienced in that context it can become a gloriously sacramental, mysterious, beautifying and ennobling thing.

Sex is God's idea

The fact that this erotic poetry is right at the centre of the Bible indicates that God has both created us with, and understands, our sexual longings. He is not embarrassed by physical affection, neither should we be.

One evening in St Barnabas we had a visiting speaker who, at one stage in his talk, invited his wife to come and join him on the platform (we don't have a traditional pulpit in the church.) As his wife stepped up to him, he kissed her and said how wonderful he thought she was. While some might be unused to that sort of display of affection in a church building, we were surprised by the overreaction of one of the church members afterwards. 'When he kissed her the Holy Spirit left the church!'

Obviously there are appropriate times and places for physical affection to be expressed. But God's command to Adam and Eve was 'Be fruitful and increase in number' (Gen 1:28). He gave us the gift of sex as the means of fulfilling his command. Far from withdrawing His Holy Spirit in displeasure when a married couple are enjoying love-making, He is pleased because this enjoyment is what he intended.

Rules?

Sex is a gift from God, and it is a particularly good gift. But it comes with certain instructions from the Maker which we ignore at our peril. How can something both as wonderful and powerful as making love be tied by rules and regulations? 'Won't that spoil the spontaneity and enjoyment of it?' you might ask. Consider the following illustration.

Imagine that you have just passed your driving test and your father has given you a fast sports car. As you survey the gleaming and powerful engine you can already feel the exhilaration of speeding along the motorway, the thrill of the sudden acceleration, or the enjoyment of driving in an open-topped car along country lanes. However if you try to drive the car with no regard for the Highway Code, for example, driving on the wrong side of the road or through the red lights, it will not be long before the car is a wreck and you are in casualty.

Our heavenly Father has given us the gift of sex, which can be exhilarating, thrilling, and enjoyable. However if we try to indulge in it without reference to the rules he has given we risk disaster with the very thing he meant for our good.

Recent Studies by the Medical Research Council Social and Public Health Sciences Unit in Glasgow, in which 7,000 third year students were involved, supports the idea that early sexual intercourse is often regretted. A third of schoolgirls and more than a quarter of boys who have had sex told researchers they regretted it. Girls said that being pressurised into sex by their boyfriends was one reason for regret. Boys said they wished they had not put pressure on their girlfriends. Thirteen per cent of the girls said they wished it had not happened at all. Britain has the highest rate of teenage pregnancies in Europe with 9,000 girls between 13 and 15 becoming pregnant each year, half of whom have abortions.

Exclusive to Marriage

It seems clear throughout Scripture that sexual intercourse is intended to be between a man and woman who have made a lifetime covenant relationship with one another and in the eyes of society. In Bible times this would have involved both parties ceremonially leaving the parental home and setting up home in a new tent. This relationship was to be life-long and exclusive. This was not easy to achieve. Many honest Bible stories tell of the unhappiness that resulted from a husband taking more than one wife, or taking another man's wife.

Abraham was happily married to Sarah. Evidently she was beautiful. King Abimelech of Gerar fancied her! (Gen 20) They had known the provision and protection of God in a number of difficult circumstances as they sought to obey him. There was one continuing point of conflict in their marriage. They were unable to have a baby. God had promised they would father a nation, but the first child was proving impossible to conceive!

Sarah's solution was to find a second wife for Abraham. 'The LORD has kept me from having children. Go, sleep with my maidservant; perhaps I can build a family through her.'(Gen16:2) Even though this had been Sarah's idea the result of that sexual union was great unhappiness, especially in the lives of the two women. Pride, jealousy, rejection, and cruelty all began to destroy their relationships. It is no wonder that the child born into this tension was destined for an unhappy life. 'He will be a wild donkey of a man; his hand will be against everyone and everyone's hand against him, and he will live in hostility toward all his brothers.'(Gen16:12) (In our society some forms of surrogacy might lead to exactly the same sort of inter-family tension.)

What would once have been called immorality is today called serial monogamy. It is now common practice for couples to sleep together on a first date (although they would never dream of sharing a bank account!) Sex screams at us from advertising hoardings, magazine racks, and television. It is not surprising that many young people find themselves lured, tempted, and cajoled into sexual encounters outside of the marriage bond. Many men and women today embark on marriage with a history of sexual experience with other partners or having had a sexual relationship with the person they eventually marry. But we are foolish to believe we can live outside the rules and not suffer the consequences. One of these consequences is that sex within marriage becomes tense, difficult, or boring.

Francis and Cathy had been going through a difficult time in their marriage. It had always been rather stormy. He had had a number of sexual encounters before marriage and sex was never easy between them. They never felt able to ask for help or counsel. She fell pregnant with their second child. She withdrew emotionally and physically while she was carrying the growing child in her womb and he found himself more and more isolated. The baby was stillborn. They each withdrew further as they tried to come to terms with their grief. One day he had a fling with an attractive work colleague. The next day he was shocked and mortified. In his despair he confessed his adultery to his wife. She was furious and heartbroken. The marriage died, and divorced followed.

It is not true that every sexual difficulty within marriage is the result of previous sexual encounters. Nor is it inevitable that where this has happened there will be long-lasting difficulty in having sex. Our God is able to bring healing and release from past experiences. Normally this will involve confession, forgiveness, and the healing ministry of His Spirit.

As you read this book God may highlight things in your sexual past before marriage of which you are still ashamed. Or it may be that you are aware that your attitude to sex has been so powerfully framed by things in our society that you have unhealthy expectations of sex within your marriage. If that is the case we suggest you should pray along these lines.

Prayer

Heavenly Father, thank you for the precious gift of (name of spouse) in marriage.
Thank you too for your wonderful gift of sex.
I admit before you now that I have abused your gift of sex in the past.
Please forgive me.
In so doing I have sinned against others and against my marriage partner.
Please forgive me.
Please cleanse me now by the blood of Jesus.
Please set me free from harmful links with people in my past.
Please heal what has been damaged by the power of your Holy Spirit.
Only you can restore holiness to my life as I give myself to (spouse) in love. I ask for your blessing on our marriage in and through the name of Jesus Christ,
Amen.

This is a wonderfully freeing prayer. However if you find yourself still burdened by feelings of guilt, it may be a good idea to ask a Christian pastor to pray with you as you make your confession. He may then lay hands on you as a sign that God has indeed the power and the will to take the guilt away.

Unfortunately an increasing number of adults have been abused sexually as children. They may 'feel' guilt when they are not in any way to blame and so it would be inappropriate to pray the prayer above in such a case. However the memory of an experience of this kind in the past can sometimes remain buried until later when it spoils the joy of lovemaking within marriage. It is not the place of this small book to address the subject of past sexual abuse, but we would strongly recommend that you seek help if this is has actually happened to you. There are many good books written to help those with a damaged past and we particularly recommend the writings of Mary Pytches and Leanne Payne. We have seen God heal scores of people from the scars of their broken past as they have been prayed for in the power of the Holy Spirit. Be encouraged! God has the power to heal and He will free all those who ask Him to do so.

Don't give up making love!

The church in 1st century Corinth was set in a society which was as obsessed by sex as our own Western society at the beginning of the 21st century. The pressure to be sexually active was probably as great then as now. So Paul wrote

'But since there is so much immorality, each man should have his own wife, and each woman her own husband. The husband should fulfil his marital duty to his wife, and likewise the wife to her husband. The wife's body does not belong to her alone but also to her husband. In the same way, the husband's body does not belong to him alone but also to his wife. Do not deprive each other except by mutual consent and for a time, so that you may devote yourselves to prayer. Then come together again so that Satan will not tempt you because of your lack of self-control.'(1Cor 7:2-5)

Not every religious leader was saying that sex was good. Some were suggesting that the most spiritual attitude to sex was to abstain. Paul refers to this misconception when he instructs Timothy how to oversee the church in godless and immoral Ephesus; 'They forbid people to marry and order them to abstain from certain foods, which God created to be received with thanksgiving by those who believe and who know the truth.'(1Tim 4:3) At times in Christian history the church has fallen into the same trap of teaching that abstinence is the greatest form of godliness. Origen had himself castrated in the third century, and Augustine talked about the 'shame' attached to sexual intercourse.

God has created us as sexual beings. He has created us with an appetite for sex. Marriage is the place for that appetite to be satisfied.

There are some similarities and some dissimilarities with our appetite for food. Those who go on hunger strike or who fast for long periods of time discover that after a certain length of time they no longer feel hungry. If we abstain from sex for too long in our marriages the same thing can happen. We may no longer feel the desire so urgently. If we keep abstaining from sex we are missing out on one of the things God has said will build our relationship. Instead we are building a vulnerability into it - someone outside the marriage might awaken the dormant sex-drive. Paul hints at the temptation that will come to a married person if they have an unfulfilled sex life. A man who is married, but is no longer making love to his wife, may be more easily led by Satan to enter into a sexual liaison outside marriage. The dreaded affair is not far from anyone who has lost the joy of sex within marriage.

If you have not been making love for some time to your spouse now is the time to admit your lack of desire. Just as after a fast you cannot eat a full gourmet meal but have to take liquid and food in small amounts initially so too with sex. You may have to gradually re-enter a physical relationship through gentle caressing touch, and progressive erotic restimulation before full intercourse and simultaneous orgasm can be enjoyed.

According to research carried out at Wilkes University, USA making love twice a week can boost your immunity to common illnesses by 30%. But beware - the effect disappears if you have sex three or four times a week!

What's wrong with us?

Sex seems so wonderful for everyone else doesn't it? Television, the press, and films all imply that everybody is always doing it and whenever they do the earth moves! In our experience this is not the case with most married couples. There is even some evidence from surveys to suggest that married people actually make love less frequently than unmarried people. Forbidden fruit has always had an allure and for some this excitement of premarital sex is lost once the marriage is contracted.

The first experience of sexual intercourse is for most women a painful thing. But after that is overcome there is for both man and woman a great excitement about sex as they begin to explore and enjoy each other's bodies. This excitement in bed is of course affected by other things in life. Stress at work, tiredness, busyness, difficulty in other relationships, all affect a couple's ability and willingness to spontaneously throw themselves into having sex. Yet in the early stages of marriage most couples don't seem to have a problem in saying 'yes, let's'.

After the birth of a baby making love can naturally be very uncomfortable for a woman. It will be some time before she can associate pleasure with those most erotic areas of her body which have recently been in such pain. Her breasts which had previously been so important in their love-making are sore and may now be temporarily taboo to her husband. The sensitive husband will need to change his patterns of love-making for his own and his wife's sake. The various erogenous zones of her body may respond differently; although she may not want him to touch her breasts she may be more be more responsive to direct clitoral stimulation. Talking together about what they are able to enjoy is especially important during this time. Sleepless nights will take their toll physically. Added to this the responsibility of a new born infant can be all-consuming emotionally. It is no wonder that she doesn't want to make love for some weeks after the birth, and it may possibly be a year before she is ready to give herself unreservedly to her husband again. In the case of their first child the husband can easily feel left out; his wife's attention is no longer focussed on him but the baby. He will need to exercise much patience; she will need to find new ways of expressing her love for him. Both of them will probably need to assure each other that they are eagerly looking forward to their sexual enjoyment and activity being fully restored.

After a number of years and perhaps a number of babies the initial testosterone rush may subside and sex may not be as spontaneous as it was earlier in marriage. This is far more common than many realise. An insensitive husband might accuse his wife, or vice versa, of 'never wanting sex any more'. Then instead of sex being a uniting element of their marriage it becomes a major battle ground. At this point some will think there is something fundamentally wrong with their marriage. Having that thought in your mind makes it even more difficult to enjoy each other's bodies.

 At bedtime the amorous husband prepared two aspirins and a glass of water for his wife.
'What's this for?' she asked.
'For your headache, darling.'
'But I don't have a headache.'
'Good!'

Our society hates to admit to having problems over sex. Because we are products of our society which venerates sex we find it hard to admit to a problem in this area of our lives. Sadly some Christian couples put a spiritual veneer on their difficulties and start thinking that its not important to have sex any longer, because there are more 'spiritual' things to get on with. Nothing could be further from the truth. Making love is one of the best forms of spiritual warfare to resist Satan's attempts to destroy Christian marriages. (see 1Cor 7:5) If you are having difficulty, the admission of this is the start of discovering help. Even the simple discovery that others are going through the same thing enables us to realise that our marriage is not as abnormal as we had previously thought.

Many marriages go through stages of dissatisfaction with the sexual relationship because of the changes in our lives as we grow older. If these are acknowledged, discussed, prayed through and thereby successfully negotiated there will be an even greater enjoyment of both sex and marriage. It has been said that 'You only have to be a dog to copulate with many different partners in your life - you have to be a sensitive human being to give and receive sexual satisfaction with one other person for the rest of your life.' This is sex as God intended it and we want to share a few ideas about how to keep your sex life developing so that it does bring you and your spouse increasing satisfaction not just in your bedroom, but in a way that permeates the whole of your relationship.

Tick those statements you agree with and put a cross against those you disagree with.

	Him	Her
1. *Sex is important for our marriage's health*		
2. *My spouse finds me sexually attractive.*		
3. *We have sexual intercourse often enough.*		
4. *We talk openly about what we enjoy in love-making*		
5. *The man should be the one to take the initiative in love-making*		
6. *Our sex life is dull and predictable*		

Vive la difference

We have already discussed the fact that men and women are made differently and nowhere is this more apparent than in our attitudes towards our sexual life. Men think of the act of intercourse and orgasm when talking about sex. Women approach the subject within the context of affectionate touch, kissing, cuddling, and arousal. This difference tends to affect the way we function as sexual beings as well. Someone has used the illustration of kitchen cookers to describe the way men and women make love! Men are like gas cookers. When they are turned on there is instant heat and they cool down immediately they are turned off. Women are more like electric cookers, which take ten minutes to warm up and then retain their heat after cooking is complete.

 ## What sex is your computer?

As you are aware ships have long been characterised as being female. 'Steady as she goes'. Should we refer to computers the same way?

Recently a group of computer scientists (all male) gave five reasons for believing computers are female.

1. No one but the creator can understand their internal logic.

2. The native language they use to communicate with other computers is incomprehensible to everyone else.

3. The message 'bad command or bad file name' is about as informative as 'if you don't know why I'm mad at you, then certainly I'm not going to tell you.'

4. Even your smallest mistakes are stored in long-term memory for later retrieval

5. As soon as you make a commitment to one you find yourself spending half your pay cheque on accessories for it.

However another group of all female computer scientists think that computers should be referred to as male, for these reasons.

1. They have a lot of data but are still clueless.

2. They're supposed to help you solve problems but half the time they are the problem.

3. As soon as you commit to one you realise that if you had waited a little bit longer you could have obtained a better model.

4. In order to get their attention you have to turn them on.

5. Big power surges knock them out for the rest of the night.

More than orgasm

We need to allow for these differences in each other. The husband may find that five minutes making love and achieving orgasm is completely satisfying, whereas his wife has not even had the time to be fully aroused in the five minutes, and is left feeling isolated as her husband is falling asleep beside her. She would probably prefer to take time over the whole evening with affectionate cuddles on the sofa, preceding more intimate and intense activity where she can come to orgasm simultaneously or even before her husband. In busy lives it is not always easy to find the time for this. Because the quick session is unfulfilling and the extended session is impossible to schedule making love can soon lapse. It may be a help to develop an understanding of one's sexual needs by referring to gourmet sex, (the extended multiple orgasm variety), and fast food sex (the quick session). There is a need for both and if a couple realise this they can plan accordingly to make sure that neither husband nor wife goes hungry!

Plan it

One of the best pieces of advice we were given was to plan a weekly date to make love. Although this sounds mechanical it has been a real help for us as the pace of life has quickened. It is all too easy to drop exhausted into bed at the end of another long day muttering a hurried good night before falling asleep. Rob Parsons in his witty book 'The Sixty-minute Marriage' (Hodder & Stoughton 1997) recommends 'If a man wants a wild Friday night he had better start working on it on Monday morning'. Most men do not have a difficulty thinking about it, but they may have difficulty planning it.

If there is a special date night always in the diary, both husband and wife can plan for it throughout the day. Cuddles, special glances and whispers of love, telephone calls and internet messages could all be part of the build-up. Wearing special underwear (under your work clothes, of course!) or a seductive perfume during the day, planning a candle-lit meal as soon as the children are in bed, dressing up alluringly for dinner, can all play a significant role. These things are really important for a woman's enjoyment of the whole sexual experience. In contrast a man is predisposed to think only about what he is hoping to get at the end of evening in bed, and may underestimate the power of this type of foreplay. In courtship a man willingly woos his beloved, and she naturally spends time beautifying herself in order to attract him. If we stop doing these things when we get married we will quickly lose the sense of excitement we knew before. Keep wooing and keep attracting each other!

As you like it

'What is and isn't allowed in lovemaking?' is a question we are sometimes asked by Christians who are married or about to get married. Making love is all about giving one's partner pleasure and so it stands to reason that we need to know what pleases our spouses. Lovemaking is also about two people enjoying each other together; if one of the partnership has a difficulty then it will affect the enjoyment of both. For this reason restraint may be needed so that both partners can continue to give themselves unreservedly. Oral sex is a case in point. If this practice is a complete turn-off for his wife, then a wise husband will concentrate on giving her pleasure another way. Any means of giving pleasure that does not hurt or repulse one's spouse is acceptable. The important thing is to be able to talk together about what you do or don't like, without feeling threatened, or made to feel guilty. That is the purpose of the following questionnaire which ends this chapter. You may like to answer it separately in the first instance and then compare notes discussing some of the issues raised together.

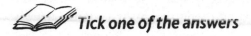 **Tick one of the answers**

Him   Her

1. I prefer sexual intercourse

In bed under the covers in the dark

On the bed with some lights on

On the floor with lights on or off

Anywhere our imagination takes us

2. Sexual arousal without climax is in my opinion

Frustrating

A special expression of love

Unnatural

A regular occurrence

3. The part of lovemaking I wish would last longer is

Fore play

Pre-climax

Orgasm

Post-climax loving

4. Oral sex is

Distasteful

An uncomfortable idea

An interesting idea

A delightful idea

5. Sexually I am

Resistant

Selective

Slow

Eager

CHAPTER 8

Looking outwards

December weddings run the risk of being overwhelmed by the weather. For this one the wind was almost gale force, and guests had to run the gauntlet of intermittent showers as they converged on the church. (We were glad that both the wedding service and the reception were to be held in the same building.) Despite this it was a magnificent affair; the bride and groom were radiantly happy; the church was seasonally resplendent; various family members took part in the service; the whole church community were involved in the arrangements for the wedding feast; and the dancing continued late into the night. Perhaps, though, the highlights were the sermon and the speeches. The preacher knew the bride's family well. He reminded the newly weds of their Christian faith and exhorted them to grow in their experience of God's grace, and to go out to serve him together. In their speeches both groom and bride acknowledged all the love and prayers that their parents had invested in them, and took on the challenge to follow their parents' examples and make their new home a place of love and prayer. On reflection afterwards the bride's mother commented approvingly to us 'it was as much a commissioning service as a wedding.'

We are called to more than 'cosy twosomeness.' Antoine de St.Exupery said 'Love is not just looking at each other. Its looking out in the same direction.' This was what God had in mind right from the start. The creation story tells us that God intended human beings to enjoy all that he had created. Part of man's joy would be in his God-given task of working 'in the garden'. The 'helper' that God gives to man in his isolated state is intended not just to help him find self-fulfilment, but also to serve God by helping him complete whatever work that God has entrusted to them. The mutuality of this is expressed later in the Bible as Peter reminds husbands that their wives are 'heirs with you of the gracious gift of life'(1 Peter 3:7). We are to be partners together as we serve him as equals before God. The synergy of two people working together towards a common goal achieves more than either of them as individuals could aspire to. Tackling a common task which will benefit someone outside our marriage will actually strengthen our marriage in the end.

 A female relative arrived late for the wedding and wanted to know all about it. 'Who gave the bride away?'
'Well, any of us could have done, but we all agreed to keep our mouths shut!'

Self or God

The spirit of the age is 'self-fulfilment'. TV ratings give us a good guide as to what interests and drives people in our society. Amongst the most popular are programmes focussed on interior decoration and home improvement. Owning a home of his own has always been an Englishman's dream - we are all familiar with the saying 'The Englishman's home is his castle'. The proportion of the population who are home owners in the UK is higher than anywhere else in Europe. It has always been the case that newly weds have rightly enjoyed setting up a new home together. Sadly today the creation of a home decorated in the latest fashionable colour has become an almost all-consuming end. The disintegration of local community life in so many of our cities is in part caused by the preoccupation of many couples with the beautification of their house and garden.

One key to fulfilment in marriage is the rediscovery of this principle of serving other people, rather than just seeking our own personal happiness. We will only find true happiness in marriage if we understand that our wedding service was a commissioning service setting us apart to serve God together. There is a glorious phrase in the Anglican Prayer Book which describes our relationship with God in this way ' .....whose service is perfect freedom...' In this chapter we want to explore various ways in which a couple can learn to love and serve God together.

Discovering our call

Every person is created and called by God to serve him in a way that is unique. Our gifts and calling are given to us at birth; the discovery or release of these should give us great joy and a thankfulness to God. 'For you created my inmost being; you knit me together in my mother's womb. I praise you because I am fearfully and wonderfully made' (Ps 139:13-14). When a person becomes a Christian their full potential as human beings, stifled or stolen from them by the enemy and his destructive designs, is restored. 'For we are God's workmanship, created in Christ Jesus to do good works, which God prepared in advance for us to do.'(Eph 2:10).

In marriage God gives people the opportunity to help each other to find and fulfil His purpose for their life.

Raising children

When a child is born to, or adopted by a couple, their prime task and calling together is nurturing that precious life. The phrase 'a quiver full of children' comes from the verse in the Psalms which refers to the happiness of the man who has many children. 'Like arrows in the hands of a warrior are sons born in one's youth. Blessed is the man whose quiver is full of them.'(Psalm 127:4). Many a modern father would probably think of a quiver full as being an impossible drain on his wallet! Some fathers leave the parenting role to the mother, and in so doing miss out on the happiness that God has planned for them. 'Children are a gift from the Lord - they are a real blessing' (Psalm 27:3 GNB). Both parents need to learn how to cherish their children as a gift from God and to take their parental responsibilities seriously. We especially recommend Mark and Lindsay Melluish's book Family Time (new wine international publishing 1999). Parenting is a job which ideally involves two people - a mother and a father.

As they tackle this task together, talking over the daily concerns, praying through the problems, and planning together for the future, they will find a God-given fulfilment in their marriage. This will require considerable self-sacrifice of time, energy and money; but the long term rewards are well worth the effort. A little known Proverb puts it like this 'Children's children are a crown to the aged, and parents are the pride of their children.'(Prov 17:6)

 Q. Is it better to be single or married?

A. Single is better...for the simple reason that I wouldn't want to change no nappies...of course if I did get married I'd think of something. I'd just phone my mother and invite her over for a coffee and some nappy-changing. (Kirsten aged 10)

Childlessness?

Some couples seem unable to conceive children of their own. For many this is a source of great sorrow. God has placed in the hearts of individual human beings a desire to be involved in preserving the future of the human race. 'So God created man in his own image, in the image of God he created him; male and female he created them. God blessed them and said to them, Be fruitful and increase in number; fill the earth and subdue it.'(Gen 1:27-28). Should a couple find they are having difficulty conceiving then we encourage them not to give up praying together for children, and seeking healing prayer in the power of the Spirit. They should probably also seek medical help, even where appropriate in vitro fertilization. Here are some stories of couples we know who have resolved the issue of infertility in different ways.

Mary and Connor were having difficulty conceiving their first child. They sought prayer at the right time for conception in her monthly cycle, and now they have a lovely baby daughter. They have a special awareness that she is a gift from God. We know many other couples who have been childless and after God's intervention have had children. This is after all something that God frequently did in Bible times. Sarai, Rachel, and Hannah, three great women of faith in Old Testament times were all barren initially - but God answered their prayers and gave them children.

However not every childless couple is healed in this way. Matthew and Lucy went through a long period in which they were unable to conceive, although they frequently sought prayer. Finally they felt the Lord say to them that they should seek to adopt children. The adoption process was a considerable emotional strain, but their home group and friends encouraged and prayed for them through it all. They are now the proud parents of three small children. The struggles they went through during the adoption process have given their marriage a strength of character that seems to have equipped them well for the problems that come from having an 'instant family'.

The joy of providing for the next generation can also be

experienced by couples who have never had children to raise themselves. Alice and Paul married later in life. But they wanted to invest what God had given them into others. Their home was always open; Alice's home cooking, and Paul's fatherly wisdom were frequently sought and always generously given. They found immense joy and satisfaction in seeing others coming to Jesus as their Saviour, and growing in maturity. They had 'spiritual children' who were as indebted to them and proud of them as natural children are of their parents.

Jobs

Even if our primary task together is raising children, most of our working life is spent separately as we work in our jobs or professions. God gives each of us gifts and skills which he wants us to use for him in our working lives as much as in our family life. In a real sense our job is our mission field. One way a couple can help each other in life is through encouragement and prayer for each other in their respective 'mission fields' at work.

This is not easy if a couple have very different professions or jobs, and if they are too busy or self-focussed to listen to each other at home and stimulate each other to keep persevering with their chosen careers. Giving each other time to talk through the joys and frustrations, the pressure and opportunities at work is critical if we are to remain involved in this major part of each others lives. Unless this happens one partner may quickly begin to think that their other half is no longer interested in their life and career. And this is probably in such contrast to their courting days. Then they were naturally and deeply interested in what each other did at work. After years of marriage, and perhaps a dreary job with a dull routine, the joy of discovering what one's partner is up to can be replaced by a boredom with the constant retelling of the same old problems. It is easy to see how a man whose wife is boring him begins to find the sympathetic ear of a female colleague increasingly attractive.

James is a highly successful businessman. His wife Susan was a nurse but is currently at home raising their children. In his view she is not really interested in his job, in the pressure he constantly feels at having to work longer and longer hours, and in the frustration that he feels in not being able to give more time to the family. In her view he is unmoved by the pressure she is under as she tries to redecorate their home (alone), by the needs of the children to have their father around, and by her own desire to find herself again, now the children are old enough to go to school. They need time to sit and talk honestly about longings, and discover ways in which they can positively and practically help each other to become all that God has created them to be.

 ## Going to bed

A husband and wife were watching TV when wife said, 'I'm tired and it's getting late. I think I'll go to bed.'

She went to the kitchen to make sandwiches for the next days lunches, took meat out of the freezer for supper the following evening, checked the cereal box levels, filled the sugar container, put spoons and bowls on the table and started the coffee pot for brewing the next morning.

Then she put some wet clothes into the dryer, put a load of clothes into the wash, ironed a shirt, and sewed on a loose button. She picked up the newspaper strewn on the floor, picked up the game pieces left on the table and put the telephone book back in the drawer. She watered the plants, emptied a waste paper basket and hung a towel up to dry.

She yawned and stretched and headed for the bedroom. She stopped by the desk and wrote a note to the teacher, counted out some cash for the field trip and pulled a text book out from hiding under a chair. She signed a birthday card for a friend, addressed and stamped the envelope and wrote a quick note for the grocery store.

She put both near her purse.

She then washed her face, put on moisturiser, brushed and flossed her teeth and trimmed her nails.

Husband called out, 'I thought you were going to bed'

'I'm on my way, ' she said.

She put some water into the dog's dish and put the cat outside, then made sure the doors were locked. She looked in on each of the children and turned out a bedside light, hung up a shirt, threw some dirty socks in the wash basket and had a brief conversation with one still up doing homework.

In the bedroom she set the alarm, laid out clothing for the next day and straightened up the shoe rack. She added three things to her list of things to do tomorrow.

About that time husband turned off the TV and announced to no-one in particular 'I'm going to bed' and he did.

Prayer support

Many Christians frequently face moral dilemmas in their work. While talking with other Christian friends in the same profession may be a great help it is also an enormous support to know that your spouse is praying for you. Richard was the company secretary of a multi-national company which had grown through significant acquisitions of other companies around the world. He often found himself under pressure to fudge certain issues as takeover documents were being drawn up. He gained the strength to stand up for the truth as he shared his concerns with his wife and she committed herself to pray regularly for him. On his retirement he was commended for his integrity! Another man in a similar position refused to sign certain documents and lost his job - but he had the support of his wife who was praying through the issues with him.

In addition to this some of our sense of significance is bound up in how well we do our jobs, and the value that we believe they have.

All of us need to know someone believes in us, our abilities, and the importance of our work. Even though you may not know the intricate details of your spouse's working conditions, you are able to encourage your partner greatly by affirming your love for, and valuing of, them and praising their abilities, whether they are a high flyer or not.

Serving God in the church

Doing something together enriches a marriage. Most couples today spend their working lives apart. John and I have often reminded ourselves of the blessing it has been to be involved together in our work of leading a church. Facing the challenge of growing a church, tackling the difficulties (yes, there are some!), seeing God at work, coping with crises, watching God change lives for good, and dealing with awkward people - all this has brought us as a couple closer together and strengthened our marriage - and amazingly we have been paid for doing it!

God may not have called you to serve Him in this way because your paid employment is elsewhere. However even if your daily working life is spent in two different locations there are still many opportunities for a married couple to serve God together in and through the church. Running or hosting a mid-week house group, teaching or helping in the children's work, going out on the soup-run down-town, gathering some friends in your sitting-room to pray, being part of the music team - all these may be possibilities which would bless others and become a means of building up your marriage relationship.

Those who have just married may be tempted to give up all activities outside work and the new home, in order to concentrate on making their marriage work. There is some wisdom in this. Referring back to Moses again 'If a man has recently married, he must not be sent to war or have any other duty laid on him. For one year he is to be free to stay at home and bring happiness to the wife he has married.'(Deut.24:5) The injunction here is to stay at home in the sense of 'in the locality' rather than being abroad at war. Bringing happiness to his wife primarily involves spending time with her. It will probably also involve doing things together. For this to happen it may well be that the new couple have to consider giving up some of the roles they fulfilled as singles so that they can take on a task as a couple. For example, choosing to host a midweek group in the home gives a wonderful opportunity to learn to pray together for others, and to help to care for the members. Boundaries may have to be set so that pastoral needs don't swamp the newly weds. But learning to look out together for the needs of others can be a great way for a new couple to increase their gratitude to God for each other, and thereby deepen their relationship.

A short time after we were married we found ourselves in a position of greater responsibility in our large city centre church. Together we had to deal with wide-ranging pastoral concerns and areas of need which challenged us both. It was a time of both pressure and excitement but our marriage was strengthened as we learnt to call out to God and to face these things together.

A week after I married a young couple at my church, I received the following thank you note from the bridegroom: 'Dear Reverend, I want to thank you for the beautiful way you brought my happiness to a conclusion.'

Pray at all times

It is important for each person to take responsibility for their own spiritual growth in a marriage. The maintaining of a personal Quiet Time has been a central part of the exercising of this responsibility for us. We do this because we never want to fall into the trap of blaming each other for not growing as Christians.

From the start of our Christian lives we were both taught about the importance and value of spending time alone with God daily, in studying the Bible and in prayer. However there have been times when that is easier said than done! A new baby, sick children, job crises, moving house - all these events can be a major disruption to a routine, and a 'time alone with God' fades into distant memory! In marriage a couple have the supreme privilege of encouraging each other in the practise of prayer. 'But encourage one another daily, as long as it is called Today, so that none of you may be hardened by sin's deceitfulness.'(Heb 13:3) When a husband can baby-sit so that his wife can just sit on her own and read and pray - that is encouragement. When a wife determines to pray daily for her husband's problems at work - that is encouragement. When they can still hold hands and pray before breakfast, after the third sleepless night in a row - that is encouragement.

The season of disruptions will soon be over (children do grow up and sleep through the night!)

Currently we are individually using the same 'Bible in a Year' Reading Plan. We have found that when we are using the same plan we are able to share the insights we have discovered and ask each other questions about the passage, if it has been puzzling.

Maybe only one of you is a Christian. It is still vital for you to find time to pray privately and read the Bible if you are to grow strong in your faith. A husband who is not a professing Christian but still encourages his Christian wife to spend time with God sows more love into his marriage than a Christian husband who is insensitive to his wife's need to be alone with God sometimes.

You don't love a woman because she is beautiful, but she is beautiful because you love her. Unknown

Finding a routine

All of us need to find a routine that suits us, and a Bible reading plan that we find most helpful. But the pattern of our lives changes so frequently and quickly that we need to stay flexible enough to reschedule our Quiet Time into a new slot if necessary. Currently John normally takes the children to school in the morning while Anne reads her Bible. But when John is travelling away she spends her normal time for Bible and Prayer behind the steering wheel on the school run - so she has to be disciplined on returning home to pick up her Bible, and not the newspaper!

Holidays, or days off, can often be a dry time spiritually for this reason. The routine of the working day is gone and replaced by the easy going lifestyle of rest and relaxation. A personal time of prayer can be overlooked altogether. But talking together as you walk along the beach can develop into praying together in a way that is not possible when our working day is usually spent apart. We have found that holidays give us a chance to express our thanks to each other for 'sticking with this marriage thing' for another year. This can turn to expressing our thanks in prayer to the Lord. We also find that easier on holiday to spend time as a family praying together round the table after a meal. Many busy families find it hard to maintain family prayers on a regular basis, but holidays can become 'holy days' in this way.

Pray together

'There will be times when you just want to leap into bed and make love', said the Bishop as he prepared us for our marriage. 'Enjoy it .... but make sure that before you fall asleep you pray together!'

Sometimes a Christian whose marriage partner is not yet a believer can look enviously at the marriage of two Christians and think 'If only I were married to a Christian - it would be so much easier if I could pray with my husband like they do'. The truth is that even Christian couples don't pray together unless both partners want to do so. We have found that we want to pray together most when we are both individually seeking God. When we lose the pattern of our own time with God our desire to pray together goes.

'Why can't we pray together more?' is a complaint many a Christian wife levels against her husband. If she is too vocal about this she may drive her husband further into self-defensiveness. She may need to learn to pray privately for her husband for God to increase his desire and willingness to pray together.

Both husband and wife will probably need to realise that they have their own personally preferred style of prayer which is not the same as their partners. They will need to adapt to each other in prayer. A man may find it easiest to pray to God in the same way that he prefers to talks to another person - namely while being active rather than sitting still. We have observed that in our church prayer meetings some of the men enjoy walking to and fro while they plead with God. Sitting down puts them in a passive mode. Often a wife sits down with her husband to pray and can't understand why he doesn't say anything - it can be because he has adopted this same passive mode. Why not try walking through the park together praying as you do so?

Finding a time in the day when you can pray together for your common concerns also requires being inventive. We have often used car journeys to pray (obviously the driver has to keep his eyes open!) When children are small and the motion of the car lulls them to sleep this is sometimes the only quiet time in the day! We have also learnt to pray over the telephone, since our daily work lives are often so separate. We pray when walking together round the garden (Vicarages are often blessed with large ones!) and when sitting at the table after meals. At all these times our prayers are conversational with our heavenly Father, as we bring our thanks and needs, but as such they are expressive of our trust in Him and they draw us closer to Him and in so doing to each other. Don't think that you have to spend a long time initially - this thought has stopped many couples from every starting to pray together. One minute is better than nothing. And one minute three or four times a day adds up significantly through the week.

Some couples successfully develop the habit of praying together every night. Raising our four children has been a wonderful but at times exhausting business. Additionally one or both of us is normally out at church meetings until late into the evening. Consequently we have found our concentration span is very short at night once we are in bed. We find it hard to pray more than simple good night prayers with each other before slipping into the land of nod. However friends of ours spend a few minutes every night praying passionately for their children, their grandchildren, and extended family. Their children have left home now and they no longer have the daily ministry of serving them in practical ways. They are expressing their love for their children daily in this habit of prayer, and in so doing have also deepened their own spiritual lives together.

Successful marriage

1. One in which a woman gives the best years of her life to the man that made them so.

2. Not so much finding the right person but being the right person.

3. One in which the husband knows when to remember and a wife knows what to forget.

Phases of life

There is no doubt that we are all under different pressure at different times of life. This can radically affect the way we pray, and the time we have available for prayer. When our children were younger in their preschool phase, and especially in their waking-at-night phase, Anne found it particularly hard to get any time alone with God. And when she did find the time all she could do was think about was what she ought to be doing in the house, or simply fall asleep!

At other times of sickness, hospitalisation, depression, grief, or bereavement the human spirit is often so crushed that it is unable to articulate prayers in the free-flowing extempore way that may have previously been quite normal. At such times the Book of Psalms can prove itself to be the Bible's Treasury of Prayers. Every human emotion, from the most sublime praise of God, to the most vengeful attitude of hatred is expressed in it. Sometimes our spirits are liberated in this way as we find others who identify with us in our anger, perplexity and pain. We have discovered that reading a Psalm aloud to each other has been helpful in such circumstances.

When someone is deeply hurting inside it is hard to pray aloud even in front of a marriage partner. At such times we have prayed for each other, laying hands on each other, asking for the Holy Spirit to come and bring the comfort that is needed. We do this as a couple in the same way as we would minister to others in the power of the Spirit. And we try to avoid pushing each other to 'snap out of it'. God's healing process often takes time, and we need to give each other time within our marriages to allow God to work. The trap that some couples fall into is to put each other under pressure to 'be more spiritual'. In marriage people live in such close proximity that this sort of emotional pressure is often counterproductive - it achieves the opposite of what we hope for.

Hospitality

We express our love for God principally by serving others. This may be a surprise to us. Jesus indicated it would catch many by surprise when they were no longer able to do anything about it.

'Then the King will say to those on his right, 'Come, you who are blessed by my Father; take your inheritance, the kingdom prepared for you since the creation of the world. For I was hungry and you gave me something to eat, I was thirsty and you gave me something to drink, I was a stranger and you invited me in, I needed clothes and you clothed me, I was sick and you looked after me, I was in prison and you came to visit me.' "Then the righteous will answer him, 'Lord, when did we see you hungry and feed you, or thirsty and give you something to drink? When did we see you a stranger and invite you in, or needing clothes and clothe you? When did we see you sick or in prison and go to visit you?' "The King will reply, 'I tell you the truth, whatever you did for one of the least of these brothers of mine, you did for me.' (Matt 25:34-40).

Every family is enriched through exercising kindness, generosity and hospitality. Two people rarely bring to a marriage the same experience of hospitality from their childhood families. They will need to work together to discover what is appropriate and possible, given their backgrounds, their family commitments and other life circumstances. Failing to exercise hospitality is potentially to miss out on receiving a blessing from those we welcome into homes. 'Do not forget to entertain strangers, for by so doing some people have entertained angels without knowing it.'(Heb13:2)

If there is light in the soul,
there will be beauty in the person.
If there is beauty in the person,
there will be harmony in the house.
If there is harmony in the house,
there will be order in the nation.
If there is order in the nation,
there will be Peace in the World.

- Unknown

In our society in the UK an ever increasing number of adults live alone. Our churches have an increasing number of adult members who for a variety of reasons are not married. Many of these 'singles' would like the opportunity to be part of an extended family, either through regular visits, or even longer term stays.

When our third child was born a single friend of ours volunteered to come and help us with the children while she was between jobs, and trying to find out what God was calling her to do next. She ended up staying with us for 14 years! Our whole family was greatly blessed by having her with us - we feel as if we entertained an angel!

There are many other ways that couples can give themselves and their homes to extending the Kingdom of God. The work of New Wine amongst church leaders at St Andrew's, Chorleywood, could not have developed without the willingness of numbers of people to offer hospitality to visiting clergy who had come to see what God was doing as he brought Renewal to a local church.

There may well be some cost for us as we offer our marriages and homes to serve the Lord in these and many other ways. But the offering of our selves back to God never goes unrewarded; in fact it is only as we do that we discover how good it is to know and serve him.

'Therefore, I urge you, brothers, in view of God's mercy, to offer your bodies as living sacrifices, holy and pleasing to God - this is your spiritual act of worship. Do not conform any longer to the pattern of this world, but be transformed by the renewing of your mind. Then you will be able to test and approve what God's will is - his good, pleasing and perfect will.' (Rom 12:1-2).

 ## Looking Outwards

Work through this checklist separately and then talk together about the implications for your marriage.

	Wife	Husband

At present I feel spiritually
> Low
> OK
> High

I would like us to pray together
> Every day
> In times of crisis
> More often
> Every week

I would like to help others by
> Being a better parent
> Entertaining in our home
> Serving the poor in some way
> Having a significant job

I would like to serve God by
> Being involved in some ministry at church
> Praying on my own
> Praying for my spouse
> Studying the Bible more

I find it easiest to pray
> In the morning
> At night
> When the children are in bed
> On the way to work
> I don't find it easy!

I like praying with you
> While walking
> Before a meal
> In the car
> Sitting close together

CHAPTER 9

Managing Money

'Where did those two pictures come from?' I asked. 'I bought them yesterday. I just thought they would finish the room off nicely' said Anne defensively. 'But we didn't budget for them, and we certainly didn't discuss it together' countered John aggrieved. The tension mounted as the newly decorated bedroom which should have been an object of admiration and delight became the subject of recrimination over the purchase of the two pictures on the wall.

We had budgeted for the decoration of the room, and we had a general agreement in our marriage that neither of us would spend money on big items without consulting the other first. As far as John was concerned pictures were not in the budget, and weren't really an essential part of the redecoration. Since he had not been consulted he was now suddenly filled with anxiety that his wife might continue to pay out money on other things without his being involved in the decision. Both those issues of the specific budget for the bedroom and the general agreement to make expenditure decisions together had to be teased out before equilibrium was restored.

Issues about money can readily provoke disagreement and distrust between a married couple. A wise couple will take the time to lay down some financial ground rules in their marriage. We recently spoke to a young couple who had been married two years, and seemed to be thoroughly enjoying the experience. When asked for the secret of their happiness they replied in a rather surprising way 'We sorted our finances out at the beginning'. They had pooled their resources into a joint bank account, set up standing orders for regular out goings, cut up their credit cards, and now lived off a lump sum of cash that they withdrew weekly. Doubtless this scheme would not suit everyone, but the point is that they had worked out how to budget for their expenses and stay out of debt. This had freed them up to enjoy their marriage.

 Maybe you heard about the man whose credit card was stolen but decided not to report it because the thief was spending less than his wife did!

A Financial Plan

Developing a financial plan at an early stage in your marriage can lay good foundations for the future. Despite the advent of student loans, which leave many people in debt for a number of years during their first job, the finances of a newly married couple are probably simpler than they will be later in their marriage. Learning to budget and stay within specified financial constraints at this stage will stand people in good stead for later.

When we were married we decided to try to live off John's salary, and save Anne's. Instead of increasing our standard of living when we married we tried to live at the same standard as we had done previously. We had the luxury of having a house provided with the job, as do most Anglican clergy. There were two significant consequences. One was that we were able to save towards the cost of housing in retirement. The other was that we didn't have to adjust our standard of living again when we had children, and were for a while living on only one salary. Most won't have the privilege of having accommodation provided with their job, but careful thought about how much of your joint salaries to invest in your housing is necessary if trouble is not to be stored up for later.

We have discovered that a careful accounting of all our income and expenditure has helped us to avoid excessive worries about money. To start with John did all of this in a hand-written form in a book. Although it was a tedious process to record every payment it enabled us over time to build up a picture of our expenditure patterns. Then, when we faced unexpected costs we could see where it might be possible to cut back in order to make the necessary savings. More recently John does the accounts on the computer with a special software package designed for the task. The essence of this task is very simple. It is the modern equivalent of dividing up ones' cash and putting it into a number of different jam jars each labelled with a description of what the money would be spent on. So housekeeping, phone, gas and electricity, travel, presents, special occasions etc all have the equivalent of their jam jars in the accounts. The art is never to spend more on any account than is stored in the jar with that label!

Many people put off managing their accounts carefully and as a consequence run into all sorts of financial troubles. The sooner you start in your marriage the easier it will be. Finances get more complicated as life goes on. Children, glorious gift from God that they are, bring ever-increasing costs. The requirements of young children may range from a plethora of toys to a never-ending supply of new clothes as they outgrow or destroy their old ones. But these are nothing compared to the demands of teenagers for allowances, travel, parties, outings, and designer clothes. Student grants are a thing of the past, and parental help is essential if students are to successfully navigate their university years without amassing huge debts. And then there are weddings... and then....! So start accounting early and beat the rush!

Some people don't know where to begin to look for help with setting up a budget. If neither of you is financially literate try asking around in your church or ask your pastor if he knows someone who seems to have sorted out their personal finances and could explain it helpfully.

Jo and Janet came to us in great distress, feeling that their marriage as well as their new-found Christian faith were at straining point. As we talked, it became clear that the root of their problems was in their use of money. They had been overspending each week and now their creditors were at the door. We prayed with them remembering Paul's words 'Do not be anxious about anything, but in everything by prayer and petition, with thanksgiving, present your requests to God'(Phil 4:6). Then we all sat around the kitchen table with a big piece of paper trying to work out a budget that they could live within, and that would leave them enough to begin to pay off their debts. They left us, able to face each other again, reconciled with God their Father, and determined to 'live the plan' - and still on the same income!

When Barbara and Jim were dating, Barbara became concerned over the lavish amount of money Jim was spending on her. After an expensive dinner date, she asked her mother, 'What can I do to stop Jim from spending so much money on me?'
Her mother replied simply, 'Marry him.'

Money Worries

What is it that makes us worry so much about money? People differ in the extent of their worry, and in what they worry about. For some it is worry about the basic necessities of life. They are living on a meagre income and there are too many mouths to fill, and too much rent to pay to balance the books. They naturally worry about how they are going to make ends meet.

Others worry that they may not be able to afford to have the car repaired. Their lifestyle is such that they have become dependent on the use of a car for their transport to work, to get their children to school, to do the shopping, and to visit their friends. Without a car the management of their life would present huge practical problems.

Others worry about whether they will have enough to pay the new mortgage they have taken out. When the Vicar of their church teaches that God is honoured by those who tithe their income they feel a huge burden of guilt. They start to worry that they are no longer living as spiritual Christians do, and fear that their lack of giving will be exposed by the church and condemned by God.

Yet others worry simply because numbers have always belonged to the frightening world of maths at school. They feel money is so ruled by numbers that it is a secret world that only the initiated can enter. They steer well clear, and even panic at the thought of having to sort out their finances, plan their giving, or prepare for their retirement.

God does not want anyone to live in the trap into which such worries may lure us. The command 'do not be afraid', or a similar injunction comes 365 times in the Bible. That is one for every day of the year - perhaps to counteract the everyday worries we have! Many of these commands come in the context of fear about finance. 'Keep your lives free from the love of money and be content with what you have, because God has said, 'Never will I leave you; never will I forsake you.' So we say with confidence, 'The Lord is my helper; I will not be afraid. What can man do to me?' (Heb 13:5-6). When I first learnt this verse by heart about the Lord being my helper as a newly converted Christian I had no idea that the context was that of money. I now realise that we often over-spiritualise our use of Scripture, and categorise too many everyday problems and difficulties as spiritual attacks. God is far more practical than we usually are; knowing we worry about money He promises to provide for us and to protect us when we are in financial difficulty.

Many of us imagine that we would have no more financial worries if we just had more money. We do not see ourselves as rich enough. This seems to have nothing to do with how much money we actually have at our disposal. A survey of 132 lottery winners who had all won millions showed that nearly a hundred of them were still thinking 'I wish I had won more and had won sooner'. Obviously the gift of contentment is not handed out with the winnings.

 Men who have pierced ears are better prepared for marriage. They have experienced pain and bought jewellery!

Debt

Statistics show that 70% of marriages that break-up do so because of financial problems. The question is not primarily how much money a couple have, but how they spend what they have, and whether they can organise their budget to the satisfaction of both, and to the avoidance of debt.

Figures on debt make grim reading. In Great Britain alone there are 4 million court summons for debt every year. One in 4 adults will experience some form of credit restriction because of debt. Keith Tondeur of Credit Action, which runs a free phone help line (0800 591084), reckons that the callers' average level of debt is over £25,000 not including mortgages.

There are at least two things we can conclude from these figures. The first is that debt is a very common problem. If you are currently experiencing money worries and are amassing debt you are not alone. The sense of isolation that debt brings can be overwhelming but there are literally millions who know how it feels.

The second thing we conclude is that people don't ask for help until they are up to their necks in trouble. The whole subject of debt is one that people find hard to talk about, because it evokes feelings of shame. It is very easy to believe that no-one else has the problem and to suffer in silence while the amount of the debt increases to unmanageable proportions. If you are already in serious debt and don't know where to turn for help then a first step might be to talk to your church leader who would be able to point you to someone in the church to help you, or to an agency like Credit Action. Advice from a skilled financial counsellor has helped many to find their way out of the hole.

Using money wisely

So how should a Christian couple use their money? Someone has counted 2350 references to money in the Bible. It is apparently high on God's agenda! Such attention to it in the Bible far outweighs the attention given to it in the pulpits of our churches. Marriage agencies report that the reasons cited for marital disagreement are most often money and sex. God seems to have known that we would need help with it!

Pray

God is deeply concerned about our financial needs. He also knows that it is often at such points of need that we learn to turn to him in prayer, and trust that he will provide for us. We have been amazed at the way that God has provided for us both in small and great ways, through the generosity of family and friends, and through unexpected gifts. It has cemented our family life to be able to pray together for our needs.

When our daughters were younger, at an age when we read bed-time stories together, we all dreamt of having a sofa in their room on which we could cuddle up together to read their books. They slept in bunk beds which were difficult to sit on, and the floor was draughty. But money was tight. 'Why don't we pray for a sofa? Anne suggested one night as we were finishing the story and about to say prayers. Very simply we asked the Lord for a sofa and then we said good night. The next day Anne received a cheque in the post for £20. It was sufficient for us to scour the papers for a second-hand sofa. Having found something suitable our first words as we all sat on it together were 'Thank you Lord.'

Need, Want and Desire

Learning to distinguish between needs and wants can be tricky especially in our consumer orientated society.

 A minister's wife went shopping. When her husband came home she said she had fallen to temptation.

Husband:	What now?
Wife	I bought a lovely dress
Husband:	Couldn't you say no?
Wife	I tried it on, looked in the mirror and thought it looked very nice. The assistant said that it made me look wonderful
Husband:	Why didn't you say 'Get thee behind me Satan'?
Wife:	I did - and he said it looks wonderful from the back too!

Most of us easily manage on a lot less than we think, but when we see something pictured in a magazine we want it. Every week new catalogues plop through the letter-box onto the doormat persuading us that we really 'need' the items that they are advertising. Up till that moment we were probably completely unaware of any particular need in that area!

God promises to supply all our needs 'And my God will meet all your needs according to his glorious riches in Christ Jesus.' (Phil 4:19) Notice that the verse goes on to say that God has glorious riches. But clearly God does not intend all Christians to be wealthy in the way 'wealth' is understood in the West today. Paul said that he himself experienced both poverty and abundance. At the time of writing to the Philippians he says he is 'amply supplied'(Phil 4:18). Yet we have only to read the beginning of the letter to discover that he is writing from prison. Most of us who read this book would find it hard to imagine calling ourselves rich if we were incarcerated.

Being Thankful

Understanding the difference between need and want lies partly in our appreciation of what we do have, as opposed to our dissatisfaction with what we do not have. Paul urges us to present our needs to God with thanksgiving. We have found that as we make a habit of thanking God for all that he has given us (and as we teach our children to do the same) we are more content. As we do this our needs and wants have been brought into sharper focus, and we have a better idea of what we should be asking God for.

Needs and wants in marriage

One of the complexities of married life is discovering that something that my partner says is a need I would class as a luxury, and vice versa. Rob was surprised that his new wife 'needed' yet another bottle of foundation cream for her face; he thought she was beautiful enough, and she had already bought one that month. Karen, his wife, was equally taken aback by his need to go out with his friends once a week to buy a pint in the pub, when she was happy to spend an evening with her feet up in front of the TV. Instead of blaming each other for needless expenditure they came to realise that each had different needs that could be both afforded within their budget and offset each other's needs.

Spender or saver

It seems that people generally are divided into two categories. They are either spenders or savers. We see this in the lives of our own children, and the way they handle their pocket-money. Two of our four children hoard any money they are given in money-boxes and savings accounts. They are loath to spend it and would rather ask us as their parents for an extra hand-out to buy anything they need or really want. The other two see the glorious possibilities of purchasing power as soon as they have some money, and seem quite content to run their savings accounts on next to nothing. In order to keep the peace in a marriage it helps if we know whether we are spenders or savers. A spender married to a saver may always be in conflict when it comes to shopping. They will need to have agreed beforehand what they want to buy. Two spenders married to each other will need to ensure they keep careful accounts if they are not to go overdrawn. Two savers may not have money problems themselves but will probably need to learn how to be generous to others.

The young couple met with their Vicar to set a date for their wedding. When he asked whether they preferred a contemporary or a traditional service, they opted for contemporary.

On the big day, a major storm forced the groom to take an alternative route to the church. The streets were flooded, so he rolled up his trouser legs to keep them dry.

When he finally reached the church, his best man rushed him into the sanctuary and up to the altar, just as the ceremony was starting.

'Pull down your trousers,' whispered the Vicar.

'Uh, Reverend, I've changed my mind,' the groom responded. 'I think I want the traditional service.'

Giving

A chapter on the subject of money would not be complete without reference to giving it away. Jesus commended those he saw giving money to the temple. 'Jesus sat down opposite the place where the offerings were put and watched the crowd putting their money into the temple treasury. Many rich people threw in large amounts. But a poor widow came and put in two very small copper coins, worth only a fraction of a penny. Calling his disciples to him, Jesus said, "I tell you the truth, this poor widow has put more into the treasury than all the others. They all gave out of their wealth; but she, out of her poverty, put in everything—all she had to live on.'(Mark 12:41-44).The widow received Jesus' commendation not because she gave an enormous sum of money but because of the sacrifice she made in it.

There are probably three important questions to that we need to ask ourselves about our giving: firstly, have we started to give money to God's work? secondly, to whom should we give any money? And thirdly, how much should we give? These questions need to be discussed and agreement reached together so that neither husband nor wife resent any subsequent action.

The traditional Biblical expectation about giving is that God's people will set aside a tithe (a tenth) of their income to give to God's work. 'Bring the whole tithe into the storehouse, that there may be food in my house. Test me in this, says the LORD Almighty, and see if I will not throw open the floodgates of heaven and pour out so much blessing that you will not have room enough for it.' (Mal 3:10). Many Christians feel that this Biblical guideline of a tenth is the right proportion to give away. However a tenth of a very low income represents a lot more in real life terms than a tenth of a high income, even though the latter would be an ostensibly far greater sum than the former. If you have not budgeted yet for any giving it is sometimes an idea to start with a small proportion of your income and then plan to increase that proportion over a period of time. You can work towards giving a tenth as your circumstances change, as you get used to living on a planned budget, and as you discover God honours your decision to obey him in this matter of giving; he will provide for you and give you grace to manage on a 'reduced income'.

Some couples decide to give away a tenth after tax has been deducted. Some do the giving before tax. Some first make allowances for their accommodation expenses. In ancient Israel there was no government benefit agency, no welfare state as we might know it, and no income tax. In a sense the tithe that the Israelites paid to the priests and Levites was God's way of providing for the nation. Some Christians take this into account when doing their calculations.

If your spouse is not a Christian it is probably not possible to give a tenth of your income to the church. It is important to maintain honesty and harmony over this issue of money so you will still need to talk together about how much you are able to give. Jesus commended the poor widow in the Bible story above for giving what she could. He knows what is at your disposal and commends you too for your gift, however large or small.

Most churches have a planned giving scheme. This is the place to start. Giving your 'tithe' to your church is one of the ways of saying that you and your household are committed to the work of God in that place and are part of that spiritual family. Money collected will be distributed to the poor, to missionaries, to those in need in the church family and used in the running of the local church. God gives all of us an invitation to be involved in changing people's lives for the better, through the giving away of money. If we dream of having strong churches which have significant ministries to children, youth, families, the elderly, the poor, the sick, and the needy, and if we want to see more people coming to living faith in Jesus, we have the opportunity to turn those dreams to reality through our giving. In this way we have the chance to invest our money in things that will change lives eternally.

Whatever you do, pray about it, discuss it together and then give your gift gladly. 'Each man should give what he has decided in his heart to give, not reluctantly or under compulsion, for God loves a cheerful giver.' (2Cor 9:7).

See next page for Talking points.

 *Talking points*

A *If you had some extra money, how would you like to spend it? Put the following list in order of priority (1-10) separately and then compare and explain your lists to each other.*

Wife   Husband

1. *New car*

2. *Face and body products*

3. *Beer/other social drink*

4. *A new kitchen*

5. *Home decoration*

6. *Sports equipment (weights, club membership, etc)*

7. *Personal clothing*

8. *Clothing for the children*

9. *Holiday*

10. *Presents*

B *Are you a spender or a saver? How has this affected your attitudes to money as a couple?*

C *What decisions have you made as a couple with regard to:*

a. *separate or joint bank accounts*

b. *budgeting your income*

c. *saving*

d. *paying off any debts*

e. *giving money away*

When you have discussed this, it may help you to write a one-sentence statement together describing your goals in each of these areas.

CHAPTER 10

Enjoying Romance

Nick decided it was time to propose marriage. He spent quite some time thinking about the best way in which to do it. Having consulted his friends he enlisted their support. Some were cajoled to provide the music - a mood-enhancing piece on a cello; others were enlisted to provide the food and act as waiters; others became stage managers who laid the tables and transformed a woodland glade into a restaurant for two to eat tete a tete. He then invited his unsuspecting girlfriend, Sarah, to go for a walk with him through the woods. Her astonishment was genuine and complete. When he popped the question she couldn't but say yes to such a romantic proposal!

This scene is far more atmospheric than that of our engagement; it was contracted in a car outside a pub! Sarah's engagement is the sort of stuff that dreams are made of. John has learnt with time how to be romantic because he realises how much pleasure it brings Anne! The fashioning of dreams is part of the fabric of romantic love stories that have traditionally been part of women's magazines for decades. While many readers recognise that they are by and large an escape from reality, many at the same time long in their hearts that life could be like that for them- just once in a while at any rate! The

Oxford English Dictionary talks about romance as 'Suggestive of an idealised sentimental or fantastic view of reality; remote from experience' For Sarah the longing became the experience!

Courtship is for many a time of intense romance. 'He was so romantic when we first met' is a statement echoed by many a wife. Sadly the accompanying refrain is also equally common 'But now he hasn't got an ounce of romance left in him!' When Anne recently asked a number of people, whose marriages we admire, what kept the sparkle of romance alive in their marriage, the wives she talked to simply laughed and the husbands tended to look guilty! Even in the best marriages, it seems, we need to work at maintaining romance. Further it is the wife who most frequently expresses a desire for more romance, and the husband who withdraws from the subject under feelings of guilt and condemnation, not really knowing how to be more romantic.

 Wife: *The two things I cook best are meatloaf and apple pie*
Husband: *Which one is this?*

Why is it that romance so often seems to die at the altar as the marriage vows are pronounced? For men, romance is often the bait in the courting game. Men can certainly be romantic in order to make their catch, but once made, the effort no longer seems necessary. Marriage often arouses the nesting instinct in a woman and her energies are channelled into creating a home. It is sometimes only after a while that she realises that there is something missing in the marital relationship and then she complains! In this chapter we want to help people to answer such questions as 'Does it have to be this way? Is it possible to maintain a sense of romance even after many years of marriage? How can we restore romance to our relationship?'

Images of Romance

Picture a number of different corny scenarios that most people would describe as romantic.

A courting couple at a restaurant eating by candle light, to the background of love songs, with all the time in the world to talk about things important and trivial, gazing adoringly into each other's eyes, and oblivious to anyone else in the restaurant.

A young man arriving home early on February 14th to greet his wife with a huge bunch of red roses.

A lingering glance exchanged between a married couple across a crowded room.

A couple stealing a few moments after supper in the kitchen, to embrace and kiss each other tenderly before tackling the inevitable washing up, caught in the act by their children.

Birds singing in the Spring air, daffodils beautifying the verges, the sky irradiated by a glowing setting sun an elderly couple on a country lane holding hands all the while as they stroll back to the home they have shared for the last 40 years.

We believe that romance is not something for new lovers alone. It can be experienced at every stage of married life. Moreover it is in our opinion the spark that keeps marriage enjoyable.

If love is a choice, romance is primarily the feeling of being loved. What is it that makes all the scenes described above seem romantic? Each of them implies that the couple are taking time to treasure and express the special relationship that exists between them.

A couple newly in love have no difficult in feeling 'special' in each other's eyes. There is a natural sense of wonder at being chosen and treasured as someone's exclusive and special friend. The first kiss, meal together, gifts of flowers, holding of hands are all interpreted as romantic. However because these are the currency in which love is normally expressed they quickly lose their romantic significance. They are only deemed romantic if they successfully arouse the feelings of being special and treasured.

Bob and Margie were staying with us as they were the speakers at a conference at our church. It was Valentine's day. As soon as the afternoon meeting finished Bob said 'Quick - to the florist'. With only half an hour before the shops were due to shut we discovered a queue in the florist. The roses were disappearing fast, and we feared we might be too late. We eventually bought the last ones, and were able to arrive home laden with bouquets for our respective spouses. They were appropriately impressed, and thankful. Later that night Anne thanked me for being so romantic. Feelings of romance were far from me as I had stood in the florists fearing the worst; but feelings of romance were successfully aroused in Anne by the gift.

Such occasions as Valentine's day, birthdays and anniversaries are extra-ordinarily important, especially to most women.

 The most effective way to remember your wife's birthday, is to forget it once.

Patricia complained about Keith having lost his romantic edge. As we counselled them we asked what actions she would interpret as romantic. She immediately replied 'Well it would help if he at least gave me a card on my birthday and on our wedding anniversary.' Keith's reply was self-defensive 'My love for you isn't expressed by such trivial things as birthday cards - it is conveyed in everything I do for you through out the year. It's only the commercial world that has made such a big thing out of birthdays and anniversaries. Anyway we can't afford to keep giving each other big presents.'

Keith was failing to understand a number of important things about romantic love. Firstly, all of us have our expectations of marriage and romance shaped by our society. What we see on films, what we read in books, and what is modelled to us by our friends forms what we believe is normal. Then we begin to expect it for ourselves - if we don't experience it we feel we are missing out. If we do we experience it we feel satisfied. In our Western society there is now considerable commercial pressure for lovers to exchange cards and gifts on such occasions as birthdays, anniversaries, and Valentine's day. To let these pass without recognition will normally result in a woman feeling 'He doesn't think I'm special any longer'. Remembering them is a sure-fire way of hitting the romance buttons in your wife.

Secondly, Keith didn't realise that a romantic gift is not necessarily an expensive one. All Patricia needed to know was that Keith was still thinking about her as he did when they were in their courting days - wanting to please her with little things that said she was special. A simple gift from someone you love is sometimes worth more than an expensive one from someone you don't. Anne recalls once being given a huge bouquet of flowers from an admirer. But his love was unsought and undesired. The extravagance and generosity of the gift left her embarrassed. Extraordinarily in contrast when I first gave her a small bunch of flowers they were received as a truly romantic gift! The thing that transformed the gift was her attitude and her desire. She was grateful for the gift, and at the same time she took it as an invitation to get to know me better .

Keith's third mistake was to forget that it is probably truer in marriage than anywhere else that 'it is the thought that counts.' His thoughtlessness over things which he knew were important to his wife implied that he was no longer considering her desires and thoughts to be important. Every husband needs to know what makes his wife feel cherished, important and special. When he does he will probably be surprised that he is once again deemed romantic!

 **To do**

1. *Think separately about what makes you feel romantic*
2. *Write down how you would like your spouse to be more romantic towards you*
3. *Compare notes!*

For most of us feelings of exclusivity and tenderness which are the basis of romantic love are also aroused by the circumstances. A dinner by candlelight is quite different from the same meal in the same place under a bare strip light! A conversation in a room with lights dimmed and with soft music on the CD player is likely to be more intimate and romantic than in the same room with the TV blaring in the corner. A 10 minute walk in the summer through the park under the moonlight is more mood-creating than an hour's hike through the country park on a grey autumn day. If these things were once part of our love language its no wonder that if we no longer do them the feelings of romance are quickly lost. It only takes a little forethought, and no extra money, to do any of these things - and the rewards will be worth it!

A sense of wonder and surprise is an essential part of romance. The Oxford English Dictionary describes romance as 'a prevailing sense of wonder or mystery surrounding the mutual attraction in a love affair.'

A sense of mystery is something inherent in the Christian faith. Although we believe that God has made himself known to us in Christ we also know that this side of heaven we will only know and see a small part of the immensity of God's love for us. 'Now we see but a poor reflection as in a mirror; then we shall see face to face.

Now I know in part; then I shall know fully, even as I am fully known.' (1Cor 13:12) The discovery of and maintaining of this sense of mystery enables us to have a right attitude of awe, and worship towards God. When Paul writes to the Christians in Colossi about his life's mission he speaks about leading people into an ever deepening relationship with God using this same language of mystery. 'My purpose is that they may be encouraged in heart and united in love, so that they may have the full riches of complete understanding, in order that they may know the mystery of God, namely, Christ,' (Col 2:2). God has made us this way - mystery within relationship is an intriguing part of our humanity.

What is true of the way in which we relate to God is also true of the way in which we relate to other each other as human beings. Every human being is a sacred and mysterious person gloriously made to reflect the image of God. Because God is unfathomable every human being is in some way unfathomable also. When a couple commit themselves to marriage they make that commitment on the basis of what they know about each other already. But they are also making a commitment to get to know each other better, and to maintain that commitment come what may in their lives. Many marriages descend over a period of time to the mundane basics of living together and getting on with life. The sense of wonder and eager anticipation of more to come disappear. A creative marriage means we may well go discovering new things which we like about each other.

 Any time you see a young man opening the door of his car for his girlfriend you know that either the car is new or the girlfriend is!

Five Enemies of Romance

Routine family life

The mundane routine of everyday living is probably the No 1 enemy of romance. All too quickly the newly married couple fall into the trap of taking on the necessary roles of living in partnership. If working hours are spent apart and the pressure of keeping up with two sets of parents, friends and hobbies fills their leisure time, it is all too easy for the pressure of life to squeeze out any time alone together. The romantic trysts of the courtship phase are no longer a feature of married life, and it is easy for a couple to be too busy to spend even an evening a week just getting to know one another better. They may even feel guilty for doing so because both parents and friends want to maintain regular contact with the new couple too.

Once children arrive on the scene the pace really hots up! There are a host of new tasks to be performed: the laundry mountain rises, housework multiplies, there may be a house-move and consequent redecoration, and careers blossom and make new demands. The daily routine seems a far cry from the carefree days pre-marriage when a trip to the cinema to sit in the back row for a cuddle was still a possibility!

When the children start school there seems to be a constant round of ferrying them to friends for tea, piano lessons and sports clubs. Babysitting is expensive and the chances of an evening in or out together look progressively more bleak since when mum is out, dad is in with the children or vice-versa!

And so it continues - we are left wondering whether we shall ever recapture the headiness of those early courting days. The secret of cultivating romance is to recognise it's value, and plan for it, learning how to be romantic within the confines of the stage that we find ourselves in. This will take determination, forethought and imagination, but it will be worth it in order to keep our marriage alive and well. Someone has said that the best gift we can give our children is a happy marriage. In order to maintain the spark in our relationship, we may need to diary in our weekly date, save up for a good babysitter, or use the time that the children are out to do something fun together instead of the household tasks. (Then teach the children to help clean up the kitchen or tidy the garden when they return!)

 What is the difference between vision and sight?

When my wife gets dressed up to go out, she looks like a vision and when she wakes up in the morning she's a sight.

Job pressure

We need to realise that the trend of modern life is away from relationships and towards achievement. In a recent article about a well-known personality who was described as the highest paid woman on TV, she outlined her typical day as follows:

6.30am	Get up, shower, grab a piece of toast, kiss husband and kids and go!
7.30am	Drive to studios, work on laptop, use mobile phone, do programme
12noon	Record voice over for a video
1pm	Grab a salad and cup of tea
1.30pm	Meeting
2.00pm	Another show
6.00pm	Home to change - parent's meeting at school

7.00pm	Dinner with husband and children
8.00pm	Kiss children good night, write weekly column, reply to fan mail
10.00pm	Write notes for new project, check diary for following day
11.15pm	Hit the pillows and straight to sleep!

Although this is the breathless schedule of a high-achiever, it is still for some reason held up as something to aspire to, and is probably not so far removed from the experience of many today in somewhat humbler jobs! Reading it, one wonders how a marriage can survive on so little time spent together (not to mention the children!) Maintaining the spark in our marriage relationship will take time. We shall both have to decide to make time- and in doing so we shall be swimming against the tide.

Taking each other for granted

When there are so many things to be done in a day, it is very tempting to just put one's head down and plough through the list of chores until it is completed. Of necessity the tasks will be divided up between the couple, and we can easily come to expect and presume that our spouse is doing their share. In so doing we take the efforts of our partner for granted, never stopping to thank, to admire, to encourage or to listen because we are too caught up in our own affairs. It is as if we are two engines running on parallel tracks never meeting at any point. Familiarity breeds contempt, as the saying goes. If one partner feels taken for granted the thought of romance is difficult to say the least.

Anger

Because we are both imperfect and unique as human beings, there will be many opportunities throughout our married lives for the expression of irritation and even anger. Habits that were endearing in a new sweetheart can become a source of aggravation in later married life. If we do not tackle the underlying issue at stake and deal with it satisfactorily, our unresolved anger can become the thing that most successfully kills off any attempts at romance! A husband who goes to bed angry, and unwilling to talk about the reason for it, will not be able to respond to his wife appearing in her most alluring negligee. However if they talk over the cause of the irritation later, and he apologises making up is enhanced by a favourite meal together, a bouquet of flowers or a special and tender card written to affirm love.

 'Every day you look lovelier and lovelier, and today you look like tomorrow' Anon.

Sometimes a pattern of anger has become deeply ingrained and threatens the marriage and the family. In this case professional counsel and deliverance prayer may be needed to heal the angry person.

Sharon and Geoff are one such couple. His angry outbursts led him to assault his wife and as a consequence she and their two small sons lived in fear. Sharon finally separated from him after he started breaking up the furniture in the family home. But the story is not finished yet. As a result of the prayers of his wife and friends, as well as professional counselling for his anger, Geoff is now on the road to recovery. He has a better understanding of himself, has committed his life to Jesus Christ in repentance and faith, and has been able to start seeing his children again. This is an extreme case but there are many occasions when the prayers and advice of a respected Christian friend or a pastor have helped to resolve a situation of anger and stalemate in a marriage.

Crisis

At times of crisis such as bereavement, accident, redundancy or sickness it goes without saying that romantic thoughts are not foremost in one's mind. However this is the time when a marriage that has been built on a foundation of true love can come into its own. The qualities that are called for include commitment, understanding and compassion. Coping with a crisis drains all one's emotional resources and leaves people with very flat or depressed feelings. If romance is to do with feelings it is not surprising that in times of crisis there is normally little opportunity or space for romantic feelings to be aroused; this energy is already taken up fire-fighting the crisis. If one person is more affected than the other, for instance through bereavement, then extra care and sensitivity will be called for in their partner to allow the necessary time for God to restore normal feelings of romance. Reaffirming love by word and touch are important at a time such as this.

Five Romantic Ideas

Flowers

Many a woman's heart has been touched by a bunch of flowers but it's a wise man who discovers what her favourites are!

A man at the door bearing one red rose wrapped in cellophane is very romantic (and he hasn't broken the bank either!)

A father who is accompanied by his young son, when he goes to the florist to buy flowers for his wife, teaches him the importance of the romantic gesture too.

Candles

Candle lit dinners 'a deux' are a byword for romance but candles are just as effective in the bedroom, and along with some room fragrance may entice a tired husband into lovemaking! 'I have perfumed my bed with myrrh, aloes and cinnamon.'(Proverbs 7.17)

A scented bath surrounded by candles is a romantic welcome home for a weary worker.

Turn the TV off, open a bottle of wine and drink it by candlelight - a much more romantic evening!

Try a summer evening picnic by candlelight - (the garden will be great when there is no babysitter available!)

Notes

Leave love messages on notes, cards (cut out pictures from used birthday cards) where your loved-one might find them unexpectedly - in his brief-case, sock drawer or shaving mirror. On her pillow or on the door-mat when she's due home.

Develop your own language to communicate romantic messages and keep them a secret between the two of you.

Special outings

Paris in the spring is every lover's destination apparently, but there are plenty of other places that can be just as romantic. Plan a special outing together or plan a surprise trip. Get the children involved in the planning (but not if it's a surprise and you want to keep it that way!) - they may have preferences about the babysitter and their activities while you're away! They will feel much happier about you going if they have had a hand in preparing for 'mum and dad's special trip'. Diary in time together doing something that you both enjoy - then enjoy the anticipation of it as well. Do something different together. If you drive everywhere by car go for a bus-ride on the top deck! Remember too that spontaneity is part of romance so don't overfill the diary so that there is no space for the spontaneous romantic activity.

Music

'If music be the food of love - play on!' wrote Shakespeare. Music is often a component part of a romantic setting. The string trio that played for our friend's proposal of marriage added enormously to the scene. The right background music to your picnic, your evening in with a bottle of wine and a candle or your bath together - even if the music comes from the CD player - will greatly enhance the romance of the occasion. Develop a collection of favourite pieces, put them together on a tape so that you can play them on trips away.

Of course many of these ideas may leave you and your partner cold. The important thing is that you discover what it is that your partner deems romantic - and get on with it! One young wife, who worked shifts as a nurse, confided that her husband often had a hot water bottle tucked into her side of the bed for when she returned home late. For her that spelled caring love and romance. However another woman, on hearing about the hot water bottle, was aghast at the idea and pronounced that it would be an immediate 'turnoff'! Husband: make sure you know your own wife's tastes. Wife: remember to thank him when he has been romantic.

A mother out shopping with her three children caught sight of the display in the window of a lingerie store. 'Do you think Daddy would like that?' she asked, pointing to a lacy negligee set.

'No way', her horrified son replied, 'Daddy would NEVER wear that!'

Conclusion

In the Oxford English Dictionary a romantic person is defined as someone who is imaginative, visionary and idealistic. The hard knocks of life often beat these qualities out of us. Try sitting down together and dreaming again. Don't be nostalgic, and don't let it be dominated by 'if onlys' and 'buts'. You probably have many years of married life ahead of you, and, even if you have fallen into some rather unromantic patterns of life, there is no absolute reason why that has to continue. Inertia is probably your biggest barrier to overcome. But by reading this far in the book there is obviously something in you that is making you want to rediscover the dreams of your earlier years. Dream on.

It may seem odd to finish a book on marriage with a few simple suggestions on how to recapture romance. Of course marriage is not only about romance. We hope that you have worked your way through the book and understood some of the principles about developing your marriage relationship. As you talk together about the marriage that you want to build romance will rise. You will be forming the foundations of a healthy and constantly growing friendship which is at the heart of every good marriage.

Romance in a marriage is like the final stage of redecorating a room. The hardest part of redecoration is the preparation work of stripping the old wallpaper, filling the cracks in the plaster, and rubbing down the window frames. The fun part is applying the final coat of paint and putting in the new furniture. Then you can sit back and enjoy the new ambience with great satisfaction at thinking 'we've done it.' If you have put the hard work in earlier in the book, then restoring romance is about the final decoration which you can then really enjoy together.

Unless the hard work of preparation is done the newly decorated room soon begins to loose its appeal as the paint begins to flake off and the cracks start reappearing in the walls. Many a couple enjoy a romantic couple of years of marriage and then the cracks begin to appear in their relationship. Soon the romance too begins to die. If that has begun to happen for you don't despair. If you work at the things we have talked about in previous chapters you will find that romance can be rekindled.

We believe that God wants people to enjoy the marriage he has given them in every way imaginable throughout their lives. He intends every couple to enjoy being together socially, physically, emotionally, spiritually, and romantically. He has made us male and female, gloriously different from each other, yet wonderfully compatible too. Growing closer to each other is a very enriching God-given adventure. Thank God again for the privilege of being invited by God and your spouse, to embark on this adventure, and pray together that God will give you the grace to enjoy the next phase of your married life even more than the one you have just been through.

We finish with the Biblical reference inscribed inside our wedding rings, which we have frequently prayed together over the years. The words give us great strength as we believe that our God knows all our needs and has our very best interests on his heart both now and for ever.

'May the God of peace provide you with every good thing you need in order to do his will, and may he, through Jesus Christ, do in us what pleases him. And to Christ be the glory for ever and ever! Amen.' (Hebrews 13:21)

Vision

To equip and encourage churches throughout the nation to reach their communities with the gospel of Jesus Christ and his Kingdom, by being continuously renewed by the Holy Spirit.

Core values

Local Church life that is welcoming, relational, accessible for all generations, and builds community and family life.

Intimate Worship that is accessible, passionate, joyful, inspiring, culturally appropriate and facilitates encounter with God.

Anointed Leadership that is visionary, courageous, humble, consistent, full of faith, and releases church members into their God-given ministries.

Strategic Mission that is holistic, inspired and empowered by the Spirit, concerned with justice and care for the poor, and encourages new church planting initiatives.

Orthodox Theology with doctrine and morality founded on the Bible and the person, teaching and work of Jesus Christ.

Bible-based Teaching and training that is interesting, thoughtful, and equipping for everyday life and ministry.

Committed Discipleship that models Christian love, prayerfulness, holiness, integrity, accountability, humility and generosity, and enables us to serve like Jesus.

Every member ministry that is gift-orientated, life transforming and expresses God's love and power.

New Wine, 4a Ridley Avenue, Ealing, London W13 9XW, England
Tel: 020 8567 6717 www.new-wine.org

New Wine Networks, c/o St Barnabas Church, Holden Road, London N12, England.
Tel: 020 8343 6130